Reading
Connections 4

From Academic Success to Everyday Fluency

Andrew E. Bennett

HEINLE
CENGAGE Learning™

Australia • Brazil • Japan • Korea • Mexico • Singapore • Spain • United Kingdom • United States

HEINLE
CENGAGE Learning

Reading Connections 4:
From Academic Success to Everyday Fluency
Andrew E. Bennett

Publisher, the Americas, Global, and Dictionaries:
Sherrise Roehr
Acquisitions Editor: Tom Jefferies
Senior Development Editor: Yeny Kim
Director of US Marketing: Jim McDonough
Senior Product Marketing Manager: Katie Kelley
Academic Marketing Manager: Caitlin Driscoll
Director of Global Marketing: Ian Martin
Director of Content and Media Production:
Michael Burggren
Senior Content Product Manager:
Maryellen E. Killeen
Senior Print Buyer: Mary Beth Hennebury

Images: All images: (c) istockphoto.com

For product information and technology assistance, contact us at
Cengage Learning Customer & Sales Support, 1-800-354-9706

For permission to use material from this text or product,
submit all requests online at **www.cengage.com/permissions**
Further permissions questions can be emailed to
permissionrequest@cengage.com

ISBN-13: 978-1-111-34865-6
ISBN-10: 1-111-34865-0

Heinle
20 Channel Center Street
Boston, MA 02210
USA

Cengage Learning is a leading provider of customized learning
solutions with office locations around the globe, including
Singapore, the United Kingdom, Australia, Mexico, Brazil and
Japan. Locate your local office at
international.cengage.com/region

Cengage Learning products are represented in Canada by Nelson
Education, Ltd.

Visit Heinle online at **elt.heinle.com**
Visit our corporate website at **www.cengage.com**

Printed in Canada
1 2 3 4 5 6 7 14 13 12 11 10

Contents

Introduction

Reading Connections is a NEW five-level series designed to develop the language and fluency necessary for success in real world and academic settings.

Reading Connections 4 contains 16 units centering on interesting articles about modern topics. A variety of important themes are covered, including the environment, health, technology, and more. Units open with a series of pre-reading exercises, followed by the main reading passage and a variety of skill building exercises. Each unit concludes with a supplementary reading passage.

Audio recordings of all student book readings are available in MP3 files on audio CD. The files are available for FREE online at elt.heinle.com/readingconnections

Also available is an assessment CD-ROM with Exam*View®*, which allows teachers to create tests and quizzes quickly and easily!

The following pages highlight and explain key features of the *Reading Connections* program.

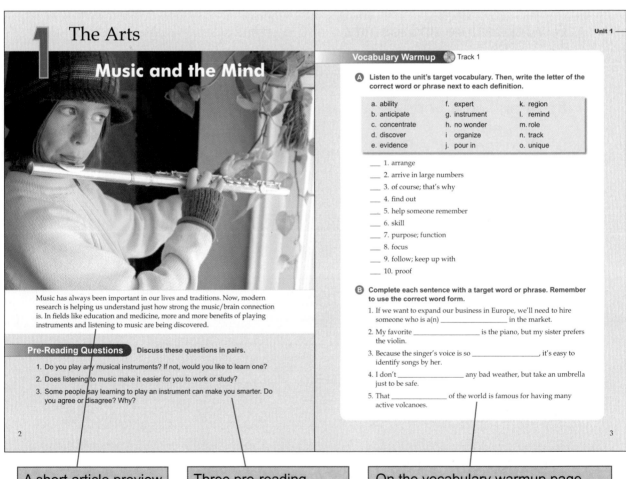

A short article preview opens the unit and helps the class prepare for the lesson.

Three pre-reading questions give students a chance to start thinking about the topic.

On the vocabulary warmup page, the unit's 15 target vocabulary items are listed. (They're also recorded on the audio CD.) Next, two sets of exercises check students' understanding of the target items.

Each reading passage is 500 words long. The unit's 15 target vocabulary items are in bold.

The reading passage is recorded on the audio CD.

Line numbers to the left of the reading passage provide an easy reference.

Part 1: Reading and Vocabulary Building

Reading Passage 🎵 Track 2

Unit 1

1   In all the world's cultures, people sing, play **instruments**, and celebrate with music. It plays such an important **role** in our lives that whole fields are dedicated to its study, including one looking at the biology of music. **Experts** are finding that because of the way our brains process music,
5   learning to play an instrument or just listening to music can have a wide range of benefits.

Music education has received a lot of attention. Learning to play an instrument can help children improve math, science, and language skills. One study in Canada **tracked** children's IQ scores for nine
10   months, **discovering** that children who studied music had the biggest test score improvements. The secret may lie in the way reading music and playing notes uses several **regions** of the brain,
15   boosting our **ability** to learn school subjects. For example, reading notes improves spatial reasoning skills, which are helpful in solving math problems like fractions.

Reading notes may be a reason why learning music improves math skills.

20   Music is also used for medical purposes, such as the treatment of diseases which affect memory. The secret lies in the way the brain processes music. One area near the forehead, the medial prefrontal cortex, connects music with memories stored in two other areas: the amygdala and hippocampus. That's why an old song can **remind** you of
25   something that happened years ago. For patients suffering from diseases like Alzheimer's, listening to music can help unlock buried memories by strengthening musical pathways to memories.

³   dedicated to – focused on; committed to
⁴   process – handle; deal with
⁹   IQ – "Intelligence Quotient" (widely used measure of intelligence)
¹⁵   boost – increase
¹⁷   spatial reasoning – the ability to mentally process shapes and patterns
¹⁹   fraction – part of a whole (ex: 1/2, 1/3)
²⁶   Alzheimer's – disease which affects memory (common amongst older people)

4

Studies of the music/brain connection often focus on classical music, since it
30   activates both the left and right sides of our brains. One study using MRI scans observed subjects' brain activity as they listened to music by composer William Boyce. It found that activity was
35   highest during the short breaks between the movements of a piece. During each pause, the person's brain **anticipated** what would come next, while **organizing** what he or she had just heard. This process of sorting beginnings and endings is similar to the way our
40   brain organizes information. It may explain why classical music can help improve memory.

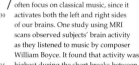
A controlled, relaxed environment helps music listeners.

Some people are taking the brain/music connection to another level by listening to personalized "brain music." First, a person's brainwaves (which are **unique** to each of us) are measured. Then, using a
45   mathematical procedure, the brainwaves are turned into short pieces of music. Listening to a "relaxing" piece (based on slower brainwaves) can slow one's heart rate and lower one's blood pressure. A person's "activating" piece (based on faster waves) can help a person **concentrate** and prepare for a difficult task.

50   It's amazing how attuned our brains are to music. Some scientists like Daniel Levitin even think we're born with the ability to learn music, just as we all have the skills to learn language. After all, children without any training frequently make up songs while they play. With the **evidence** of music's benefits **pouring in**, it's **no wonder** countries like Japan and
55   Hungary make music study a part of their education systems. People are recognizing that more than just a form of entertainment, music is also great for the brain.

³⁰ activate – turn on; make active
³¹ MRI – Magnetic Resonance Imaging (device showing an internal image of a patient)
³³ composer – person who writes music
³⁶ movement – section of a piece of classical music
⁴² personalized – specially made for somebody
⁴⁵ procedure – method; sequence
⁵⁰ attuned to – sensitive towards; focused on
⁵³ make up – create

5

Beneath the reading passage is a simplified glossary. To the left of each glossary item is the line number where it can be found.

A caption beneath each image shows its relevance to the article.

Following the passage are five reading comprehension questions including main idea, detail, vocabulary, and analysis questions.

These vocabulary exercises check students' knowledge of the unit's 15 target vocabulary items. There are three types of exercises: synyonym, fill in the blank, and word form.

Reading Comprehension — Choose the best answer.

Main Idea

1. ( ) What is the main idea?
   A. Music therapy is effective in treating Alzheimer's patients.
   B. The human brain is difficult to understand.
   C. Besides being enjoyable, music has real-world applications.
   D. It's best to learn music at a very young age.

Detail

2. ( ) In the Canadian study, which children had increased IQ scores?
   A. Those who had always played music
   B. Those who studied music for a period of time
   C. Those who already had high IQs
   D. Those who could not play an instrument

Vocabulary

3. ( ) In line 32, what does "observed" mean?
   A. heightened   B. watched
   C. preserved   D. composed

Analysis

4. ( ) Why may classical music help our memories?
   A. Listening to it uses processes we also use to record memories.
   B. Classical music is easier to play than other types of music.
   C. It activates the left side of our brain, but not the right side.
   D. Brain activity is highest when we listen to music being played.

5. ( ) What can we infer about "brain music"?
   A. It may not be effective in treating disease.
   B. Listening to the music is only helpful to those who excel at math.
   C. Everybody's musical recording is different.
   D. It does a better job helping people relax than helping them focus.

Short Answers — Answer each question based on the article.

1. How can reading music make us better at math?

2. What parts of the brain store memories?

3. How are a person's brainwaves turned into music?

These three questions are also based on the reading passage. Answers should be one sentence long.

Vocabulary Building

A Choose the answer that means the same as the word or phrase in italics.

1. The police do not usually arrest someone without *evidence* that the person has committed a crime.
   A. range   B. activity   C. proof

2. Airports can *track* planes all the way from take off to landing.
   A. follow   B. suffer   C. celebrate

3. In that *region* of the country, the temperature often falls to 10 degrees below zero.
   A. movement   B. attention   C. area

4. Considering all the money they're losing, it's *no wonder* they're going out of business.
   A. so unfortunate B. very recent   C. not surprising

5. Computers are great at helping people *organize* digital photos.
   A. relax   B. sort   C. concentrate

B Complete each sentence with the best word or phrase. Remember to use the correct word form.

instrument	pour in	role	unique	ability

1. After the scientist won the Nobel Prize for chemistry, job offers and research opportunities _____.

2. The gallery sells _____ works of art from Mexico.

3. My _____ in the company is making sure shipments arrive on time at their intended destinations.

4. People do not have the _____ to breathe underwater.

5. Orchestras include string _____ such as the violin, cello, and viola.

C Circle the correct form of each word.

1. (Anticipate/Anticipation) is high that the swimmer will set a new record.

2. The person who (discovers/discovery) a new planet can also name it.

3. The procedure requires total (concentrate/concentration), so the operating room must be kept very quiet.

4. The watchmaker (expertly/expert) reassembled the antique clock.

5. The website can send you a (remind/reminder) of your important appointments.

6

7

vi

Improving knowledge of word parts is an excellent way to strengthen reading skills. In this section, three word parts (one prefix, one root, and one suffix) are presented. They're based on word parts found in the reading passage. A short exercise checks students' knowledge of the material.

Three discussion questions give students a chance to talk about the topic. Some questions are based on the reading passage. Others, which are more general, are based on the unit's larger theme.

Part 2: Focus Areas

Focus on Language

Word Parts

Study the word parts in the chart. Then, read the following pairs of sentences. Circle if the second sentence is true or false.

Word Part	Meaning	Examples
pre-	before; in front of	preface, preview
-form-	shape	informal, performance
-ful	full of	colorful, cheerful

1. The study's preliminary results show people love the product.
   It's the final set of results from the study. (True / False)
2. Sandra's political ideas don't conform to those of her classmates.
   Sandra and her classmates have different political views. (True / False)
3. Mr. Lee is well known in the community for being truthful.
   People in the community think Mr. Lee is honest. (True / False)

Grammar *Adjective Clauses*

We use adjective clauses to provide more information about a person, place, or thing. Depending on the type of noun being modified, the connector *who, whom, which,* or *that* is used.

person	who, whom, that	Ex: Lisa is the person who can help you.
place	where	Ex: This is the place where I was born.
thing	which, that	Ex: The CD that you want is over there.

Combine the two sentences using an adjective clause.

1. Toronto is a great city. You can find some excellent restaurants there.

2. This is a delicious fruit. It only grows in these mountains.

3. I'd like to introduce you to my friend. She works as a research assistant.

8

Focus on Production   Unit 1

Talk About It   Discuss these questions in small groups.

1. The article discusses several benefits of learning instruments and listening to music. Which do you think are the most important? Why?
2. What types of music may work best for helping people with medical problems? Are there any types which would be less suitable?
3. Do you agree that people are born with the ability to learn music? Why or why not?

Write About It

Question: Should every child learn to play a musical instrument? Give two reasons to support your opinion. Prepare by writing notes on the lines below. The first few words of the paragraph are written to help you get started.

Opinion: _____

Reason 1: _____

Reason 2: _____

In my opinion, learning an instrument is _____

9

This section presents practical grammar structures with the goal of improving communicative grammar skills. First, a short, simple explanation is given. That's followed by structural models (if applicable) and example sentences. Finally, a short exercise checks students' ability to apply what they've learned.

In this guided exercise, students write a paragraph about the topic. Several lines are provided so students can create a mini-outline. The first few words of the paragraph are also given. Paragraphs should be short (less than 10 sentences long). Though there is no single "correct" answer, a model paragraph is provided in the answer key on the website.

From unit to unit, this section alternates between a short conversation and a short listening passage. Every conversation and listening passage includes three of the unit's target vocabulary items, for recycling purposes.

The audio script can be found on the website.

The final page of each unit contains a supplementary reading passage. This 250-word article provides a deeper insight into certain aspects of the unit's topic.

The conversations and short listening passages are recorded on the audio CD.

The article is recorded on the audio CD.

Focus on Testing

Listening   Listen to the conversation. Then, answer the following questions.

 Track 3

1. ( ) What is the woman's occupation?
    (A) Graphic designer   (B) Shift manager
    (C) Physical therapist   (D) Sales associate

2. ( ) What is the woman concerned about?
    (A) Her pay   (B) Her new colleague
    (C) Her health   (D) Her workload

3. ( ) What does the man suggest doing?
    (A) Hiring another person
    (B) Quitting the job
    (C) Listening to soft music
    (D) Talking to the boss

Reading   Read the article. Then, answer the following questions.

For people looking for a unique gift for that special someone, Custom Creations might have the answer. The firm employs a dozen professional songwriters who can write a personalized song just for you. For a reasonable fee, you can have an original piece of music dedicated to your husband, wife, parent, or child.

Ted Simmons, the firm's CEO, has been writing lyrics for more than 20 years. He started out writing songs for commercials, movies, and pop singers. Then, anticipating a rise in the customized gift market, he founded Custom Creations. According to Mr. Simmons, his firm has written more than 2,000 songs and has brought countless smiles to clients' faces.

1. ( ) How many people work at Custom Creations?
    (A) 1   (B) 12
    (C) 20   (D) 2,000

2. ( ) The word "founded" in paragraph 2, line 4, is closest in meaning to
    (A) located   (B) purchased
    (C) established   (D) imagined

3. ( ) What did Ted Simmons do early in his career?
    (A) He built movie sets.
    (B) He was a professional songwriter.
    (C) He worked at a custom gift shop.
    (D) He sang in a band.

10

Unit 1

Supplementary Reading - *Physical Brain Changes*   Track 4

The benefits of music for academic learning are well documented, thanks to research tracking young people's progress as they learn an instrument. Evidence is also mounting that studying music leads to actual physical changes in one's brain development. Significantly, the amount of activity in certain regions of the brain, as well as the structure of specific areas, is altered by learning and playing music.

One study at the University of Munster in Germany monitored the brain activity of two groups of people between 20 and 30 years of age. One group consisted of 20 musicians who had played music for at least 15 years. The other group consisted of 13 non-musicians. Each participant listened to a recording of piano music as the researchers monitored their brain responses. While listening to the recording, the musicians showed 25% more activity in the area of the brain that processes auditory signals. Although the music was from a piano, the response level was higher for all musicians, whether they played the piano, violin, or another instrument.

A separate study at McMaster University in Canada followed the progress of 12 children for a year. Six of the children were taught music using the Suzuki method, a popular teaching method from Japan. The other six did not learn an instrument. Over the course of the study, the researchers took regular measurements of certain brain regions. They found that the music students had increased activity in the region of the brain responsible for focusing attention and making sense of different sounds.

Read each sentence. Circle if it is true (T) or false (F).

1. The article offers examples of the medical uses of music.   T / F
2. The German study included more musicians than non-musicians.   T / F
3. In the German study, brain activity was measured as people listened to music.   T / F
4. The study involving the Suzuki method took place in Japan.   T / F
5. The McMaster study was conducted over a 12-month period.   T / F

11

From unit to unit, this section alternates between a short reading passage (such as an article, e-mail, report, etc.) and a cloze passage. Every reading passage recycles three of the unit's target vocabulary items.

Five true and false questions check students' comprehension.

Scope and Sequence

	Theme	Reading Skills	Word Parts	Grammar	Test Preparation
1	The Arts	Identifying the main idea and details; using vocabulary in context; making inferences	**prefix:** pre- **root:** -form- **suffix:** -ful	Adjective Clauses	**Listening:** Conversation about work **Reading:** Article about a company
2	Culture	Identifying the main idea and details; using vocabulary in context; making inferences	**prefix:** com- **root:** -flu- **suffix:** -al	The Passive Voice	**Listening:** Announcement at a museum **Reading:** Cloze passage article
3	The Environment	Identifying the main idea and details; using vocabulary in context; recognizing suggestions	**prefix:** re- **root:** -cycl- **suffix:** -less	Not only... but also	**Listening:** Conversation at a library **Reading:** Letter about an offer
4	Space	Identifying the main idea and details; using vocabulary in context; recognizing implications	**prefix:** under- **root:** -sci- **suffix:** -able	Such as + gerund	**Listening:** Speech about a new agency **Reading:** Cloze passage article
5	The Internet	Identifying the main idea and details; using vocabulary in context; recognizing implications	**prefix:** in- **root:** -ven(t)- **suffix:** -ant	Present Perfect	**Listening:** Conversation about a colleague **Reading:** Advertisement for a service
6	Identity	Identifying the main idea and details; using vocabulary in context; recognizing suggestions	**prefix:** ex- **root:** -tract- **suffix:** -wards	Comparative Adjectives	**Listening:** Announcement on a plane **Reading:** Cloze passage article

	Theme	Reading Skills	Word Parts	Grammar	Test Preparation
7	Health	Identifying the main idea and details; using vocabulary in context	**prefix:** con- **root:** -plic- **suffix:** -ment	Despite & In spite of	**Listening:** Conversation about an inspection **Reading:** News report
8	Entertainment	Identifying the main idea and details; using vocabulary in context	**prefix:** per- **root:** -rupt- **suffix:** -ure	Subject-Verb Agreement & Prepositional Phrases	**Listening:** Report about housing **Reading:** Cloze passage biography
9	Nature	Identifying the main idea and details; using vocabulary in context; recognizing intentions	**prefix:** be- **root:** -duc(t)- **suffix:** -ate	Parallel Structure	**Listening:** Conversation at an aquarium **Reading:** Want ad for an assistant
10	Business	Identifying the main idea and details; using vocabulary in context; recognizing suggestions	**prefix:** bene- **root:** -vert- **suffix:** -ive	Present and Future Conditional	**Listening:** Announcement at a store **Reading:** Cloze passage article
11	Law and Crime	Identifying the main idea and details; using vocabulary in context	**prefix:** tele- **root:** -cour- **suffix:** -ee	Past Perfect	**Listening:** Conversation about a delivery **Reading:** News report
12	Social Issues	Identifying the main idea and details; using vocabulary in context; recognizing implications	**prefix:** dis- **root:** -found- **suffix:** -logy	Reduced Adjective Clauses	**Listening:** Speech opening a conference **Reading:** Cloze passage article

	Theme	Reading Skills	Word Parts	Grammar	Test Preparation
13	Growing and Aging	Identifying the main idea and details; using vocabulary in context; making inferences	**prefix:** pro- **root:** -dict- **suffix:** -eer	So...that	**Listening:** Conversation at a press conference **Reading:** Announcement about an event
14	Science and Technology	Identifying the main idea and details; using vocabulary in context; recognizing differences	**prefix:** trans- **root:** -cred- **suffix:** -ion	Noun Clauses	**Listening:** Store helpline recording **Reading:** Cloze passage article
15	Globalization	Identifying the main idea and details; using vocabulary in context; analyzing characteristics	**prefix:** en- **root:** -equ- **suffix:** -ness	Along with, Besides, & In addition to	**Listening:** Conversation - apologizing **Reading:** Article about NGOs
16	The Future	Identifying the main idea and details; using vocabulary in context; making inferences	**prefix:** alter- **root:** -fac(t)- **suffix:** -ent	Used to	**Listening:** Report about new research **Reading:** Cloze passage article

1

Music and the Mind

Music has always been important in our lives and traditions. Now, modern research is helping us understand just how strong the music/brain connection is. In fields like education and medicine, more and more benefits of playing instruments and listening to music are being discovered.

Pre-Reading Questions   Discuss these questions in pairs.

1. Do you play any musical instruments? If not, would you like to learn one?

2. Does listening to music make it easier for you to work or study?

3. Some people say learning to play an instrument can make you smarter. Do you agree or disagree? Why?

Vocabulary Warmup 💿 Track 1

A Listen to the unit's target vocabulary. Then, write the letter of the correct word or phrase next to each definition.

a. ability	f. expert	k. region
b. anticipate	g. instrument	l. remind
c. concentrate	h. no wonder	m. role
d. discover	i organize	n. track
e. evidence	j. pour in	o. unique

_____ 1. arrange

_____ 2. arrive in large numbers

_____ 3. of course; that's why

_____ 4. find out

_____ 5. help someone remember

_____ 6. skill

_____ 7. purpose; function

_____ 8. focus

_____ 9. follow; keep up with

_____ 10. proof

B Complete each sentence with a target word or phrase. Remember to use the correct word form.

1. If we want to expand our business in Europe, we'll need to hire someone who is a(n) _____ in the market.

2. My favorite _____ is the piano, but my sister prefers the violin.

3. Because the singer's voice is so _____, it's easy to identify songs by her.

4. I don't _____ any bad weather, but take an umbrella just to be safe.

5. That _____ of the world is famous for having many active volcanoes.

3

Part 1: Reading and Vocabulary Building

1   In all the world's cultures, people sing, play **instruments**, and celebrate with music. It plays such an important **role** in our lives that whole fields are dedicated to its study, including one looking at the biology of music. **Experts** are finding that because of the way our brains process music,
5   learning to play an instrument or just listening to music can have a wide range of benefits.

Music education has received a lot of attention. Learning to play an instrument can help children improve math, science, and language skills. One study in Canada **tracked** children's IQ scores for nine
10   months, **discovering** that children who studied music had the biggest test score improvements. The secret may lie in the way reading music and playing notes uses several **regions** of the brain,
15   boosting our **ability** to learn school subjects. For example, reading notes improves spatial reasoning skills, which are helpful in solving math problems like fractions.

Reading notes may be a reason why learning music improves math skills.

20   Music is also used for medical purposes, such as the treatment of diseases which affect memory. The secret lies in the way the brain processes music. One area near the forehead, the medial prefrontal cortex, connects music with memories stored in two other areas: the amygdala and hippocampus. That's why an old song can **remind** you of
25   something that happened years ago. For patients suffering from diseases like Alzheimer's, listening to music can help unlock buried memories by strengthening musical pathways to memories.

---

³ dedicated to – focused on; committed to
⁴ process – handle; deal with
⁹ IQ – "Intelligence Quotient" (widely used measure of intelligence)
¹⁵ boost – increase
¹⁷ spatial reasoning – the ability to mentally process shapes and patterns
¹⁹ fraction – part of a whole (ex: 1/2, 1/3)
²⁶ Alzheimer's – disease which affects memory (common amongst older people)

Studies of the music/brain connection often focus on classical music, since it activates both the left and right sides of our brains. One study using MRI scans observed subjects' brain activity as they listened to music by composer William Boyce. It found that activity was highest during the short breaks between the movements of a piece. During each pause, the person's brain **anticipated**

A controlled, relaxed environment helps music listeners.

what would come next, while **organizing** what he or she had just heard. This process of sorting beginnings and endings is similar to the way our brain organizes information. It may explain why classical music can help improve memory.

Some people are taking the brain/music connection to another level by listening to personalized "brain music." First, a person's brainwaves (which are **unique** to each of us) are measured. Then, using a mathematical procedure, the brainwaves are turned into short pieces of music. Listening to a "relaxing" piece (based on slower brainwaves) can slow one's heart rate and lower one's blood pressure. A person's "activating" piece (based on faster waves) can help a person **concentrate** and prepare for a difficult task.

It's amazing how attuned our brains are to music. Some scientists like Daniel Levitin even think we're born with the ability to learn music, just as we all have the skills to learn language. After all, children without any training frequently make up songs while they play. With the **evidence** of music's benefits **pouring in**, it's **no wonder** countries like Japan and Hungary make music study a part of their education systems. People are recognizing that more than just a form of entertainment, music is also great for the brain.

---

30 activate – turn on; make active
31 MRI – Magnetic Resonance Imaging (device showing an internal image of a patient)
33 composer – person who writes music
36 movement – section of a piece of classical music
43 personalized – specially made for somebody
45 procedure – method; sequence
50 attuned to – sensitive towards; focused on
53 make up – create

........**Main Idea**

1. (   ) What is the main idea?
   A. Music therapy is effective in treating Alzheimer's patients.
   B. The human brain is difficult to understand.
   C. Besides being enjoyable, music has real-world applications.
   D. It's best to learn music at a very young age.

........**Detail**

2. (   ) In the Canadian study, which children had increased IQ scores?
   A. Those who had always played music
   B. Those who studied music for a period of time
   C. Those who already had high IQs
   D. Those who could not play an instrument

........**Vocabulary**

3. (   ) In line 32, what does "observed" mean?
   A. heightened   B. watched
   C. preserved   D. composed

........**Analysis**

4. (   ) Why may classical music help our memories?
   A. Listening to it uses processes we also use to record memories.
   B. Classical music is easier to play than other types of music.
   C. It activates the left side of our brain, but not the right side.
   D. Brain activity is highest when we listen to music being played.

5. (   ) What can we infer about "brain music"?
   A. It may not be effective in treating disease.
   B. Listening to the music is only helpful to those who excel at math.
   C. Everybody's musical recording is different.
   D. It does a better job helping people relax than helping them focus.

Short Answers   Answer each question based on the article.

1. How can reading music make us better at math?

   _____

2. What parts of the brain store memories?

   _____

3. How are a person's brainwaves turned into music?

   _____

Vocabulary Building

A Choose the answer that means the same as the word or phrase in italics.

1. The police do not usually arrest someone without *evidence* that the person has committed a crime.
   A. range   B. activity   C. proof

2. Airports can *track* planes all the way from take off to landing.
   A. follow   B. suffer   C. celebrate

3. In that *region* of the country, the temperature often falls to 10 degrees below zero.
   A. movement   B. attention   C. area

4. Considering all the money they're losing, it's *no wonder* they're going out of business.
   A. so unfortunate   B. very recent   C. not surprising

5. Computers are great at helping people *organize* digital photos.
   A. relax   B. sort   C. concentrate

B Complete each sentence with the best word or phrase. Remember to use the correct word form.

instrument	pour in	role	unique	ability

1. After the scientist won the Nobel Prize for chemistry, job offers and research opportunities _____.

2. The gallery sells _____ works of art from Mexico.

3. My _____ in the company is making sure shipments arrive on time at their intended destinations.

4. People do not have the _____ to breathe underwater.

5. Orchestras include string _____ such as the violin, cello, and viola.

C Circle the correct form of each word.

1. (Anticipate/Anticipation) is high that the swimmer will set a new record.

2. The person who (discovers/discovery) a new planet can also name it.

3. The procedure requires total (concentrate/concentration), so the operating room must be kept very quiet.

4. The watchmaker (expertly/expert) reassembled the antique clock.

5. The website can send you a (remind/reminder) of your important appointments.

Part 2: Focus Areas

Focus on Language

Word Parts

Study the word parts in the chart. Then, read the following pairs of sentences. Circle if the second sentence is true or false.

Word Part	Meaning	Examples
pre-	before; in front of	preface, preview
-form-	shape	informal, performance
-ful	full of	colorful, cheerful

1. The study's preliminary results show people love the product.
   It's the final set of results from the study. (True / False)

2. Sandra's political ideas don't conform to those of her classmates.
   Sandra and her classmates have different political views. (True / False)

3. Mr. Lee is well known in the community for being truthful.
   People in the community think Mr. Lee is honest. (True / False)

Grammar *Adjective Clauses*

We use adjective clauses to provide more information about a person, place, or thing. Depending on the type of noun being modified, the connector *who, whom, which,* or *that* is used.

person	who, whom, that	Ex: Lisa is the person who can help you.
place	where	Ex: This is the place where I was born.
thing	which, that	Ex: The CD that you want is over there.

Combine the two sentences using an adjective clause.

1. Toronto is a great city. You can find some excellent restaurants there.

   _____

2. This is a delicious fruit. It only grows in these mountains.

   _____

3. I'd like to introduce you to my friend. She works as a research assistant.

   _____

Talk About It   **Discuss these questions in small groups.**

1. The article discusses several benefits of learning instruments and listening to music. Which do you think are the most important? Why?

2. What types of music may work best for helping people with medical problems? Are there any types which would be less suitable?

3. Do you agree that people are born with the ability to learn music? Why or why not?

Write About It

Question: Should every child learn to play a musical instrument? Give two reasons to support your opinion. Prepare by writing notes on the lines below. The first few words of the paragraph are written to help you get started.

Opinion: _____

Reason 1: _____

Reason 2: _____

In my opinion, learning an instrument is _____

_____

_____

_____

_____

_____

_____

_____

_____

Listening

Listen to the conversation. Then, answer the following questions.

Track 3

1. (   ) What is the woman's occupation?
   (A) Graphic designer   (B) Shift manager
   (C) Physical therapist   (D) Sales associate

2. (   ) What is the woman concerned about?
   (A) Her pay   (B) Her new colleague
   (C) Her health   (D) Her workload

3. (   ) What does the man suggest doing?
   (A) Hiring another person
   (B) Quitting the job
   (C) Listening to soft music
   (D) Talking to the boss

Reading

Read the article. Then, answer the following questions.

For people looking for a unique gift for that special someone, Custom Creations might have the answer. The firm employs a dozen professional songwriters who can write a personalized song just for you. For a reasonable fee, you can have an original piece of music dedicated to your husband, wife, parent, or child.

Ted Simmons, the firm's CEO, has been writing lyrics for more than 20 years. He started out writing songs for commercials, movies, and pop singers. Then, anticipating a rise in the customized gift market, he founded Custom Creations. According to Mr. Simmons, his firm has written more than 2,000 songs and has brought countless smiles to clients' faces.

1. (   ) How many people work at Custom Creations?
   (A) 1   (B) 12
   (C) 20   (D) 2,000

2. (   ) The word "founded" in paragraph 2, line 4, is closest in meaning to
   (A) located   (B) purchased
   (C) established   (D) imagined

3. (   ) What did Ted Simmons do early in his career?
   (A) He built movie sets.
   (B) He was a professional songwriter.
   (C) He worked at a custom gift shop.
   (D) He sang in a band.

Supplementary Reading - *Physical Brain Changes* Track 4

The benefits of music for academic learning are well documented, thanks to research tracking young people's progress as they learn an instrument. Evidence is also mounting that studying music leads to actual physical changes in one's brain development. Significantly, the amount of activity in certain regions of the brain, as well as the structure of specific areas, is altered by learning and playing music.

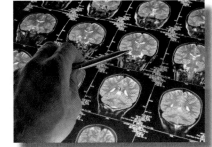

One study at the University of Munster in Germany monitored the brain activity of two groups of people between 20 and 30 years of age. One group consisted of 20 musicians who had played music for at least 15 years. The other group consisted of 13 non-musicians. Each participant listened to a recording of piano music as the researchers monitored their brain responses. While listening to the recording, the musicians showed 25% more activity in the area of the brain that processes auditory signals. Although the music was from a piano, the response level was higher for all musicians, whether they played the piano, violin, or another instrument.

A separate study at McMaster University in Canada followed the progress of 12 children for a year. Six of the children were taught music using the Suzuki method, a popular teaching method from Japan. The other six did not learn an instrument. Over the course of the study, the researchers took regular measurements of certain brain regions. They found that the music students had increased activity in the region of the brain responsible for focusing attention and making sense of different sounds.

Read each sentence. Circle if it is true (T) or false (F).

1. The article offers examples of the medical uses of music. T / F

2. The German study included more musicians than non-musicians. T / F

3. In the German study, brain activity was measured as people T / F
   listened to music.

4. The study involving the Suzuki method took place in Japan. T / F

5. The McMaster study was conducted over a 12-month period. T / F

2 Culture

Body Language Across Cultures

Our body language, such as our facial expressions, says a lot about us. It communicates our feelings even when we don't say a word. Just as languages differ from country to country, so does body language. Understanding those differences is important for cross-cultural communication.

Pre-Reading Questions   Discuss these questions in pairs.

1. What are some common hand gestures? (ex: the "OK" sign) What do they mean?

2. Is your body language expressive? In other words, is it easy for other people to tell what mood you're in even when you don't say anything?

3. Can you think of some examples of body language from other cultures that are different from your own?

Vocabulary Warmup Track 5

A **Listen to the unit's target vocabulary. Then, write the letter of the correct word or phrase next to each definition.**

a. avoid	f. expressive	k. posture
b. aware of	g. gesture	l. refer to
c. communicate	h. intensely	m. sequence
d. embarrassment	i. muscle	n. tend to
e. encourage	j. opposite	o. vary

____ 1. totally different

____ 2. extremely; passionately

____ 3. usually act a certain way or do a certain thing

____ 4. know about

____ 5. interact; share information

____ 6. motion (ex: pointing)

____ 7. way of standing; body position

____ 8. shame

____ 9. keep away from

____ 10. the way a series of things is ordered

B **Complete each sentence with a target word or phrase. Remember to use the correct word form.**

1. During the speech, the inventor _____ some of the people who influenced his work.

2. Fruit and vegetable prices _____, depending on the current supply, weather, and crop forecasts.

3. Every year, the university _____ people to visit the campus by offering free tours.

4. After playing baseball for three hours, all my _____ were sore.

5. Mr. Hoshizaki has such a(n) _____ face that it's easy to tell what kind of mood he's in.

Part 1: Reading and Vocabulary Building

Reading Passage ⊙ Track 6

1   Using words isn't the only way we say things. By leaning forward, narrowing our eyes, and folding our arms, we also **communicate** feelings. With as much as 70% of what we say coming from this type of non-verbal communication, it's clearly important to be **aware of** our

5   body language. That's especially true when dealing with people from other cultures, since a smile in Baltimore may not mean the same as a smile in Beijing.

    There are several types of body language. With **gestures**, we use our arms and hands to show moods, ask questions, and share information.

10   Our faces are very **expressive**, with more than 90 **muscles** working to send messages of surprise, happiness, anger, and so on. There's also kinesic communication, which **refers to** our body shape. By walking in a slumped

15   position, we show we're sad, while a straight **posture** displays confidence. Other types of body language include our tone of voice, clothing, and proxemics (the physical distance

20   between people).

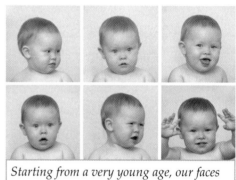

Starting from a very young age, our faces are very expressive.

    Since body language differs greatly from place to place, it's easy to misunderstand what someone from another country means. For instance, smiling, one of the most common expressions, is used to show happiness or friendliness in North America. Yet in East Asia, it can

25   be a sign of discomfort or **embarrassment**. Also, shaking one's head may mean "no" in England, while carrying the **opposite** meaning in Bulgaria. Many daily actions, from greeting people to shaking hands, **vary** around the world.

---

⁴ non-verbal – unspoken or unrelated to speaking
¹² kinesic – related to one's body
¹⁴ slumped – bent over
²⁵ discomfort – the state of not feeling well
²⁶ carry – have; hold

Culture has a strong influence on non-verbal communication. The simple
30   act of looking someone in the eye is not at all that straightforward. In the
USA, people are **encouraged** to look directly at people when speaking to
them. It shows interest in what they're saying and is thought to carry a
sense of honesty. However, in Japan
and Korea, people **avoid** long periods
35   of eye contact. It's considered more
polite to look to the side during
a conversation. The Lebanese, in
contrast, stand close together and
look **intensely** into each other's eyes.
40   The action shows sincerity and gives
people a better sense of what their
counterpart wants.

*Common gestures and actions, such as
daily greetings, differ around the world.*

Given such differences with even the most common expressions, people
traveling abroad and those in international business have a real need to
45   learn the other culture's body language. One helpful method is watching
movies or TV shows. Picture books showing a **sequence** of events can
also illustrate concepts like personal space. In face to face contacts, if you
can't understand someone's gestures or expressions, it's a good idea to
ask what he or she means.

50   Because body language is subconscious, people **tend to** be unaware of
the messages they're sending to others. So, it's helpful to consider your
own body language before dealing with people from other cultures.
The last thing you want to do is anger a friend or lose a case over a
misunderstanding. Being knowledgeable about the body language of
55   friends, clients, and colleagues can go a long way towards improving
understanding and avoiding miscommunication.

---

[30] straightforward – clear; direct
[42] counterpart – person you are dealing with
[47] illustrate – show; give an example of something
[47] concept – idea
[50] subconscious – occurring without a person's awareness
[56] miscommunication – misunderstanding over something's meaning

..........**Main Idea**

1. (   ) What is the main idea?
    A. Most types of body language mean the same thing around the world.
    B. A gesture in North America and Asia can have similar meanings.
    C. Understanding body language improves communication across cultures.
    D. It isn't easy to make friends with people from other countries.

..........**Detail**

2. (   ) Standing very close to someone is an example of _____.
    A. a gesture
    B. kinesic communication
    C. proxemics
    D. a facial expression

..........**Vocabulary**

3. (   ) In line 40, what does "sincerity" mean?
    A. honesty   B. doubt
    C. activity   D. culture

..........**Analysis**

4. (   ) What can we infer about Bulgarians?
    A. Bulgarians may shake their heads to mean "yes."
    B. Their expressions are similar to those of people in England.
    C. Few of them shake hands when greeting people.
    D. They often smile to show their discomfort or embarrassment.

5. (   ) What method of learning about body language is NOT discussed?
    A. Watching TV shows
    B. Directly asking for meaning
    C. Taking an online course
    D. Reading picture books

Short Answers   **Answer each question based on the article.**

1. How is smiling different in North America and East Asia?

_____

2. Why do Americans look people in the eye while speaking to them?

_____

3. Who has a real need to learn the body language of other cultures?

_____

Vocabulary Building

A **Choose the answer that means the same as the word or phrase in italics.**

1. Many of my grandmother's letters include a line or two *referring to* the small town where she grew up.
   A. mentioning   B. describing   C. introducing

2. Are you *aware of* the airline's new baggage restrictions limiting us to one check-in item?
   A. supportive of   B. in compliance with   C. knowledgeable about

3. Results *vary*, but in general, people on the diet lose 10 pounds.
   A. guarantee   B. differ   C. surprise

4. To open the safe, you have to input the correct *sequence* of numbers.
   A. amount   B. order   C. authority

5. Though she is unable to speak, Dr. Cowell can *communicate* her ideas using a portable keyboard and monitor.
   A. express   B. develop   C. research

B **Complete each sentence with the best word. Remember to use the correct word form.**

posture	intensely	embarrassment	gesture	muscle

1. In France, it would be rude to make that _____ with your hands.

2. Models need to have excellent _____ as they walk down the runway.

3. Actors, used to doing crazy things, don't usually have a strong sense of _____.

4. During the last typhoon, it rained _____ for three days.

5. This machine lets you exercise both your arm and leg _____.

C **Circle the correct form of each word.**

1. My parents give me a lot of (encourage/encouragement) to follow my dreams.

2. (Avoid/Avoiding) a problem won't help you solve it.

3. The (expressive/expressively) painting does a good job capturing the artist's feelings.

4. My sister (tending to/tends to) bite her fingernails when she's nervous.

5. Place the lights there and there, on (opposite/opposition) sides of the room.

Part 2: Focus Areas

Focus on Language

Word Parts

Study the word parts in the chart. Then, read the following pairs of sentences. Circle if the second sentence is true or false.

Word Part	Meaning	Examples
com-	together	combine, compact
-flu-	flowing	affluent, superfluous
-al	related to	emotional, physical

1. There's a community of 150 shepherds in the region.
   More than 100 people live in the area. (True / False)

2. The confluence of the two rivers creates a powerful body of water.
   The two rivers flow side by side but never meet. (True / False)

3. Mr. Westwood's refusal of the promotion came as a shock to the board.
   Mr. Westwood did not accept the higher position. (True / False)

Grammar *The Passive Voice*

When we use the passive voice, we first state the object of an action. That's followed by the action itself. Then, the performer of the action may or may not be stated.

Structure: **object + be + past participle (+ by + noun)**

Ex: The votes were counted by the debate moderator.

Ex: The brochures will be delivered tomorrow afternoon.

Rewrite each sentence using the passive voice.

1. The Beatles recorded the album 45 years ago.

   _____

2. The doorman is checking the guests' names.

   _____

3. Volunteers will collect donations at the mall.

   _____

Talk About It — Discuss these questions in small groups.

1. In your opinion, what types of body language say the most about us? Gestures? Facial expressions? Posture?

2. Let's say you're about to travel to Australia. How can you learn about the country's body language?

3. Should people who study abroad or do business overseas try to change their body language to match that of the places they travel to? Why or why not?

Write About It

Question: Should the study of body language be a part of learning a foreign language? Give two reasons to support your opinion. Prepare by writing notes on the lines below. The first few words of the paragraph are written to help you get started.

Opinion: _____

Reason 1: _____

Reason 2: _____

Studying another culture's body language _____

_____

_____

_____

_____

_____

_____

_____

_____

_____

Listening Listen to the announcement. Then, answer the following questions.

Track 7

1. (   ) Where is this announcement being made?
   (A) A library
   (B) A university
   (C) A zoo
   (D) A museum

2. (   ) What are people encouraged to do?
   (A) Interact with the exhibits as much as possible
   (B) Make sure their children don't cause trouble
   (C) Take photographs, as long as a flash isn't used
   (D) Attend a lecture about becoming a scientist

3. (   ) What can people do in Section C?
   (A) Learn about fossils
   (B) Buy a present or have a snack
   (C) Pet a snow leopard
   (D) Visit the information center

Reading Choose the correct word(s) to fill in each blank.

Frequent travelers know how difficult it can be to communicate with people in other countries. Nobody can be expected to learn the language of every place they visit. (___1___), there are a number of ways to reduce problems while improving your overseas experience. First, use a guidebook, which should include a number of common phrases. Just (___2___) an effort to say "hello" and "thank you" can go a long way towards winning over locals. Small phrase books and dictionaries also tend to help at restaurants, supermarkets, and stores. Believe it or not, even a pen and piece of paper, for writing down numbers or drawing pictures, can be useful. When all else fails, use hand (___3___) to get your message across.

1. (   ) (A) Consequently   (B) However
         (C) Unfortunately   (D) Furthermore

2. (   ) (A) to make   (B) made
         (C) makes   (D) making

3. (   ) (A) gestures   (B) muscles
         (C) postures   (D) sequences

Supplementary Reading - *Robotic Body Language* Track 8

The ins and outs of body language make interacting with another person complex enough. But what if your counterpart isn't a person at all? In recent years, we've been dealing more and more with intelligent robots. They provide services like military training and medical care. Though robots' faces can be made to look human, improving their expressions, gestures, and ability to read body language remains a key challenge.

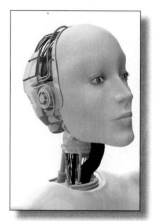

In 2009 an interesting study was conducted at Carnegie Mellon University. In the room were a robot and a table with several objects on it. People asked the robot yes/no questions to determine which object it was going to choose. It took an average of 5.5 questions for people to guess the correct item. Occasionally, the robot's eyes glanced at the item. When that happened, people needed only five questions to guess the correct object. Tellingly, the eye movement only made a difference when a humanoid robot called Geminoid was involved. It made no difference when a non-humanoid robot was used.

In addition to being more expressive, robots can also benefit from knowing how to read body language. One application where this can help is Intelligent Tutoring Systems (ITS). ITS robots are used as private tutors, teaching assistants, and training specialists. Scientists are working on ways to make them more "affect-aware." That means they can judge whether a person is interested, bored, tired, etc. Researchers at UC San Diego's Machine Perception Lab have already taught an ITS to recognize smiles. Over time, as robots learn to recognize more emotions, they'll become better at their tasks.

Read each sentence. Circle if it is true (T) or false (F).

1. Robots are already being used to train soldiers.   T / F
2. In the Carnegie Mellon study, more than one type of robot was used.   T / F
3. When Geminoid moved its eyes, people had a harder time guessing   T / F
   the object.
4. Being affect-aware means a robot can read body language.   T / F
5. At UC San Diego, scientists are focusing on ways to make robots   T / F
   more expressive.

3 The Environment

Turning Waste Into Wealth

Recycling is a key element in many companies' efforts to "go green." As they help the environment, companies are finding that yesterday's garbage can be today's profit source. Firms are coming up with ways to turn garbage into useful goods and materials.

Pre-Reading Questions   Discuss these questions in pairs.

1. What kinds of things can be recycled?

2. In general, do companies care about the environment?

3. Can you think of any ways that companies might profit from industrial waste and other garbage?

Vocabulary Warmup 🔘 Track 9

A Listen to the unit's target vocabulary. Then, write the letter of the correct word or phrase next to each definition.

a. ambitious	f. excess	k. potential
b. construction	g. from scratch	l. raw material
c. convince	h. generate	m. take notice
d. creative	i. opportunity	n. widespread
e. effort	j. policy	o. worthless

___ 1. without value

___ 2. chance

___ 3. extra; surplus

___ 4. having big goals; wanting to accomplish a lot

___ 5. common; seen in many places

___ 6. material that things are made from (ex: wood)

___ 7. produce

___ 8. get someone to agree

___ 9. guideline; procedure

___ 10. pay attention

B Complete each sentence with a target word or phrase. Remember to use the correct word form.

1. The mine has the _____ to supply us with thousands of tons of copper.

2. I made these cookies _____, using fresh ingredients.

3. My brother isn't very _____, but my sister can draw almost anything.

4. The noise from the _____ site makes it hard to think.

5. After years of losses, making the firm profitable again will take a lot of _____.

Part 1: Reading and Vocabulary Building

1   In the past, people tended to classify things as either worth something
     or **worthless**. Household, office, and industrial waste, seen as worthless,
     was usually burned or buried in landfills. However, as landfills fill up,
     the planet heats up, and energy and **raw material** prices go up, we're
5   rethinking what we consider "waste" and "pollution." New technologies
     are making it possible to reuse waste materials, and businesses are
     finding ways to not only throw away less, but to turn trash into cash.

     Recycling is the most **widespread** form of waste reuse. There are many
     benefits to recycling cans, bottles, newspapers, and other daily goods.
10   Not only does it save governments money by reducing spending on
     landfills, but it also helps companies and individuals lower garbage
     disposal costs. Also, using recycled materials to make goods is much
     cheaper than using raw materials. For instance, making a can from
     recycled cans uses 1/20 the energy required to make a can **from scratch**.
15   Cost savings like that lead to higher company profits.

     Another type of waste, organic material, has a clear economic value.
     Scientists have developed ways to turn vegetables, grains, and even
     used coffee grounds into biofuel, and companies are **taking notice**.
     Supermarket giant Sainsbury's has the

20   **ambitious** goal of turning all of its food
     waste into biofuel. In the past, the firm's
     Scotland operations used more than 300
     trucks to collect organic waste and bring
     it to landfills. Now, just one truck collects
25   the waste and delivers it to processing
     plants for conversion to biofuel. It's a win-
     win situation for the company and the
     environment.

Biofuel is already being used in vehicles around the world.

¹ classify – arrange into categories
² industrial waste – waste produced by companies, often from factories
³ landfill – place where garbage is buried
¹² disposal – throwing away
¹⁶ organic – coming from living things (such as plants and vegetables)
¹⁸ coffee grounds – crushed, used coffee beans
¹⁸ biofuel – fuel made from plants and other organic materials
²² operations – business activities

Through **creative efforts**, other waste materials are being turned into completely new products. An interesting example is EaKo, a UK-based company which makes beautiful bags and wallets from used fire hoses. On the other side of the world, a local government effort in the Philippines aims to eliminate waste altogether. Part of the effort involves turning old plastic bags and other materials into **construction** blocks. In both cases, garbage is seen not as a problem, but as a business **opportunity**.

Even factories are finding opportunities to increase profits in Earth-friendly ways. As goods are produced, factories often **generate** large amounts of heat and gas, which are then released into the air. Yet by refitting a plant, it's possible to capture these materials and turn them into energy, which the factory can then reuse. **Excess** energy can even be sold to power companies for a profit. The

Modernizing factories can lead to big energy and cost savings.

potential for this type of operation is fantastic. Recaptured energy from US factories could meet 20% of the country's power needs.

Waste reuse, in addition to its financial value, has many environmental benefits. It reduces garbage disposal costs and landfill use, while fighting global warming by lowering the amount of CO_2 in the air. Yet, businesses, who have responsibilities to investors and shareholders, tend to focus on cost benefits. When waste reuse **policies** can be shown to save or make money, it's much easier to **convince** firms to act in ways which are both eco-friendly and business friendly.

[33] aim to – plan to; have the goal of
[33] eliminate – get rid of; reduce to zero
[42] refit – upgrade by installing new equipment
[43] capture – take; grab
[51] CO_2 – carbon dioxide
[52] shareholder – owner of a company's stock
[55] eco-friendly – good for the Earth

.... **Main Idea**

1. (   ) What is the main idea?
   A. Room for new landfill sites is quickly running out.
   B. Garbage disposal costs are forcing businesses to change their ways.
   C. By reusing waste, businesses can be profitable and eco-friendly.
   D. Soon, 20% of the world's power will come from recaptured energy.

.... **Detail**

2. (   ) What does the Philippine government create with its waste?
   A. Plastic bags
   B. Wallets
   C. Biofuel
   D. Construction blocks

.... **Vocabulary**

3. (   ) In line 26, what does "conversion" mean?
   A. sale   B. support
   C. change   D. transport

.... **Analysis**

4. (   ) Why would factories want to capture gas before it's released into the air?
   A. To refit the plant
   B. To turn it into products
   C. To use the gas again
   D. To generate more heat

5. (   ) What does the article suggest about businesses?
   A. Few businesses are interested in helping the environment.
   B. Most companies want to refit their factories but can't afford to.
   C. We don't know how to convince them to change their habits.
   D. When making decisions, firms must keep investors in mind.

Short Answers Answer each question based on the article.

1. In Scotland, what does Sainsbury's do with its organic waste?

   _____

2. What does EaKo use to make its bags and wallets?

   _____

3. What are two environmentally friendly benefits of reusing waste?

   _____

Vocabulary Building

A Choose the answer that means the same as the word or phrase in italics.

1. After the sale, we'll return any *excess* stock to the warehouse.
   A. necessary   B. extra   C. defective

2. The new steel plant will *generate* 300 jobs for the community.
   A. create   B. tax   C. recycle

3. When you look over the samples, *take notice* of any tears or holes in the cloth.
   A. repair   B. arrange   C. recognize

4. The store's return *policy* entitles customers to a refund within 14 days of a purchase.
   A. rule   B. product   C. network

5. If the business plan is successful, it has the *potential* to make all the investors rich.
   A. wealth   B. possibility   C. responsibility

B Complete each sentence with the best word or phrase. Remember to use the correct word form.

from scratch	worthless	opportunity	widespread	raw material

1. When _____ prices rise, everything from shoes to chairs becomes more expensive to make.

2. Some people see losing a job as a(n) _____ to return to school for an advanced degree.

3. This car was redesigned _____, making it different from everything else on the market.

4. The phone isn't _____, but I doubt you can sell it for much.

5. At the end of the year, there are _____ discounts at shops.

C Circle the correct form of each word.

1. An (effort/efforts) is underway to restore the river to its original beauty.

2. (Construct/Construction) of the highway is expected to take two years.

3. Your presentation was (convince/convincing), but I'm not sure there's enough money in the budget.

4. His plan to become CEO within five years is very (ambitious/ambition).

5. The brochure was (creative/creatively) designed, using an original lettering style and color scheme.

Part 2: Focus Areas

Focus on Language

Word Parts

Study the word parts in the chart. Then, read the following pairs of sentences. Circle if the second sentence is true or false.

Word Part	Meaning	Examples
re-	again	reaffirm, reapply
-cycl-	round	bicycle, cyclist
-less	without	pitiless, restless

1. Those animals are able to regenerate lost body parts.
   The animals have the ability to grow back body parts. *(True / False)*

2. Because it's a cyclical industry, we experience a downturn every 10 years.
   It's normal for the business to go through hard times once a decade. *(True / False)*

3. The merciless emperor was known for treating his subjects cruelly.
   The ruler often showed pity to the people in his empire. *(True / False)*

Grammar *Not only...but also*

Often, we want to say more than one thing about a person, place, idea, etc. To do so, we can use the structure *not only...but also*.
Ex: Laura is a good salesperson. She's also a loyal employee. Not only is Laura a good salesperson, but she's also a loyal employee.
Ex: The software organizes photos. It also makes editing easy. Not only does the software organize photos, but it also makes editing easy.

Combine the two sentences using *not only...but also*.

1. It's a beautiful painting. And, it's reasonably priced.

   _____

2. The storm will damage the crops. Plus, it might flood the road.

   _____

3. I can give you directions. I can also drive you there myself.

   _____

Talk About It   Discuss these questions in small groups.

1. Should companies which are not environmentally friendly be forced to change? If so, how?

2. Would you be willing to pay more for something if it included 100% recycled materials?

3. Besides recycling, what can people do to help the environment?

Write About It

Question: Should people be fined for throwing away more than a certain amount of garbage (for example, more than 2 pounds/day)? Give two reasons to support your opinion. Prepare by writing notes on the lines below. The first few words of the paragraph are written to help you get started.

Opinion: _____

Reason 1: _____

Reason 2: _____

Throwing away a lot of garbage _____

_____

_____

_____

_____

_____

_____

_____

_____

Listening Listen to the conversation. Then, answer the following questions.

Track 11

1. (   ) Where are the people?
    (A) In an office complex   (B) In a library
    (C) At a school   (D) At a construction site

2. (   ) What does the woman think about the noise problem?
    (A) It's possible to reduce it.   (B) It's bad everywhere.
    (C) It's mostly the man's fault.   (D) It's due to the lack of laws.

3. (   ) What does the man plan to do?
    (A) Complain to the construction company
    (B) Make a suggestion to the library
    (C) Install a new set of windows
    (D) Convince the woman to change

Reading Read the letter. Then, answer the following questions.

Dear Mr. Harper,

Thank you very much for your letter. At Springfield Produce, we're always looking for creative ways to reduce waste and make ourselves more environmentally friendly. So, your proposal to convert our factory waste into biofuel certainly caught our attention.

I've discussed your plan with our board of directors, and they're willing to put it to work, on a trial basis. After half a year, we'll look at the results and decide where to go from there. Personally, I think the idea has a lot of potential, and I'm looking forward to working with you on it.

Yours sincerely,

Albert Greene

1. (   ) What is the purpose of this letter?
    (A) To respond to a complaint   (B) To accept a proposal
    (C) To ask for clarification   (D) To make an inquiry

2. (   ) What can be inferred about Springfield Produce?
    (A) They leave all decision making to Mr. Greene.
    (B) They have always converted their waste into biofuel.
    (C) They aren't concerned about the environment.
    (D) They will try Mr. Harper's plan for at least six months.

3. (   ) The word "trial" in paragraph 2, line 2, is closest in meaning to
    (A) temporary   (B) environmental
    (C) legal   (D) effective

Supplementary Reading - *Mining Garbage for Gold* Track 12

Every year, people buy hundreds of millions of cell phones, computers, and MP3 players. Using them enriches our lives, but disposing of them via landfill or incineration creates serious environmental problems. Fortunately, many electronics can be recycled. What's more, their circuit boards and chips can be mined for precious metals such as gold, silver, and palladium. Granted, the amounts are small. (It's estimated that it takes 80 computers to produce one gram of gold.) However, as tens of millions of computers are thrown away every year, it could quickly add up to a substantial amount.

Though the idea is promising, recycling old electronics can be difficult. Dismantling computers is labor intensive, requiring many screws, boards, and panels to be removed. However, more companies are designing machines so they can be easily recycled.  Furthermore, advances in metal extraction are making the process more cost effective. For instance, a research group at the Tokyo Institute of Technology has developed a way to extract gold from items like cell phones by soaking them in an organic solvent.

Some firms, like Taiwan's Super Dragon Technology Company, are already prospering by extracting valuable materials from electronics. Founded in 1996, the company has built itself into a multi-million dollar business. Ninety-five percent of the electronics come from companies such as Taiwan Semiconductor, and the other 5% are from individuals. Super Dragon is able to produce an impressive 300 to 500 kilograms of gold on a monthly basis. If environmental concerns aren't enough to drive interest in recycling electronics, numbers like that surely will be.

Read each sentence. Circle if it is true (T) or false (F).

1. Eighty grams of gold can be removed from a single computer. T / F
2. Taking a computer apart requires a lot of labor. T / F
3. The breakthrough at the Tokyo Institute of Technology makes gold extraction easier. T / F
4. Super Dragon has been recycling electronics for more than a decade. T / F
5. The majority of Super Dragon's electronics come from private individuals. T / F

4 The Search for Other Worlds

Over the last decade, space research, including the search for other planets, has become more aggressive. Several methods have been developed to locate worlds in other solar systems. Using these techniques, we may soon be able to identify other inhabited planets.

Pre-Reading Questions   Discuss these questions in pairs.

1. Do you believe there is life on other planets?

2. Once every few years, there is a big event in space (such as an eclipse) that can be seen from Earth. Do you follow these events or ignore them?

3. To support life, what characteristics does a planet need? (ex: breathable air)

Vocabulary Warmup ⊙ Track 13

A **Listen to the unit's target vocabulary. Then, write the letter of the correct word next to each definition.**

a. agency	f. indirect	k. slightly
b. atmosphere	g. inhabited	l. suitable
c. constantly	h. limitation	m. technique
d. dim	i. locate	n. underway
e. examine	j. signal	o. universe

___ 1. roundabout

___ 2. method

___ 3. restriction

___ 4. study; analyze

___ 5. find where something is

___ 6. organization; association

___ 7. already happening

___ 8. reduce the amount of light

___ 9. appropriate

___ 10. continuously

B **Complete each sentence with a target word. Remember to use the correct word form.**

1. The island is _____ by many species of insects, birds, and mammals.

2. Planets with _____ containing toxic gases are unlikely to support life on the surface.

3. After the storm, the damaged boat sent out a(n) _____ to help rescuers find it.

4. There are so many planets in the _____ that there's a good chance some of them (besides the Earth) host life forms.

5. Our new house is _____ larger than the one we used to live in.

Part 1: Reading and Vocabulary Building

1　Are we alone in the **universe**? The question has been asked countless
　times, and we may finally be close to an answer. For decades, efforts
　to find life on other planets have used passive methods such as
　listening for radio **signals** from space. More recently, scientists have
5　taken a more active role in looking for **inhabited** planets. Advances in
　telescopes and other instruments, along with many new discoveries,
　have scientists feeling confident that they'll soon have answers.

　Two key methods are used to search for "exoplanets" – that is, planets
　outside our solar system. Both use **indirect** methods by **examining**
10　stars to see if a planet is in its system. The first key **technique** is
　called the radial velocity method. It's known that planets, through
　gravitational effects, cause their stars to move around, or "wobble."
　By measuring a star's wobble, we can verify that a planet is in the
　system. This method was used to find the first exoplanet in 1995. The
15　**limitation** of the technique is it's more **suitable** for larger planets, such
　as those the size of Jupiter.

　The second key planet finding technique,
　the transit-detection method, can
　locate smaller planets similar in size
20　to our Earth. When a planet passes, or
　"transits," in front of a star, it causes the
　light from the star to **dim slightly**. Using
　advanced telescopes, we can measure that
　dimming to determine a planet's size and
25　temperature. Scientists are hopeful that
　this technique will lead to the discovery of
　many Earth-sized rocky planets.

When a planet transits in front of a star, we can learn a lot about the planet.

1　countless – a great many; impossible to count
11　velocity – speed
12　gravitational – related to the force that a body in space has over another body
12　wobble – shake or move in a circle
13　verify – determine; confirm
18　detection – discovery
27　rocky planet – planet with a hard, solid surface

Once a planet is found, steps are taken to check if it's habitable. First, it has to be the right size – between 0.5 and 10 times the Earth's mass. The
30 planet must also be in the star's "habitable zone." To be in this zone, the planet needs to be a certain distance from its star (not too close or too far away) so it can support liquid water. Then, a planet's **atmosphere** needs to be studied. It's thought that if the right group of gases – including oxygen, CO_2, and ozone – is present, the planet could be home to other
35 life forms.

Many efforts in this galactic search are **underway**. More than 30 involve telescopes on Earth. Some, like the HARPS in Chile, have made important discoveries. Other efforts, which are
40 space based, are even more promising. The COROT telescope, built by France and several other countries, was launched in 2006. It looks for rocky planets using the transit method.
45 NASA, the US space **agency**, sent the Kepler telescope into space in 2009. Its 0.95 meter-wide telescope also uses the

Telescopes in space, such as the Hubble, have many advantages.

transit method to **constantly** watch 100,000 stars.

Although these efforts are young, the results so far have been excellent.
50 Several hundred large exoplanets have been found, and scientists continue finding smaller and smaller planets. Future missions, such as Europe's Darwin mission and NASA's Terrestrial Planet Finder, plan to photograph exoplanets and study their atmospheres. Not only may we soon know the locations of other worlds, but we'll also know what they
55 look like. The future should be very interesting indeed.

---

[28] habitable – able to support life
[29] mass – physical quantity
[30] zone – area
[34] ozone – gas in the atmosphere that blocks a star's harmful rays
[36] galactic – happening in space; related to a galaxy (such as the Milky Way)
[43] launch – send into space
[52] terrestrial – similar to the Earth

.... **Main Idea**

1. (   ) What is the main idea?
    A. Scientists are working hard to find Earth-like planets.
    B. Large exoplanets are easier to find than small ones.
    C. Telescopes are becoming more and more advanced.
    D. The Kepler telescope can watch 100,000 stars at a time.

.... **Detail**

2. (   ) What do the radial velocity and transit-detection methods have in common?
    A. They are both indirect search methods.
    B. They both measure a star's dimming.
    C. They are both good at finding Earth-sized planets.
    D. They both measure gravitational effects.

.... **Vocabulary**

3. (   ) In line 40, what does "promising" mean?
    A. distant   B. expensive
    C. hopeful   D. challenging

.... **Analysis**

4. (   ) What does the article imply about the COROT telescope?
    A. It has a 0.95 meter-wide telescope.
    B. It uses both the radial velocity and transit-detection methods.
    C. It may be able to find planets the size of the Earth.
    D. It was built entirely by France.

5. (   ) Which of these planets would NOT be considered habitable?
    A. One with CO_2 in its atmosphere
    B. One whose surface is covered by ice
    C. One that is six times the Earth's mass
    D. One which is not too close to its sun

Short Answers   Answer each question based on the article.

1. When was the first exoplanet found?

_____

2. What happens when a planet transits in front of a star?

_____

3. What will future planet finding missions try to do?

_____

Vocabulary Building

A Choose the answer that means the same as the word in italics.

1. What *technique* did you use to figure out the heat of the planet's core?
   A. telescope   B. attitude   C. method

2. At some museums, children can *examine* ancient animal bones with their own hands.
   A. prepare   B. apply   C. inspect

3. After four years of research in the Peruvian mountains, the team *located* the lost city.
   A. found   B. analyzed   C. welcomed

4. Many governments have *agencies* which promote local tourism.
   A. ministers   B. travelers   C. organizations

5. The annual strawberry festival, which will last three days, is already *underway*.
   A. happening   B. crowded   C. popular

B Complete each sentence with the best word. Remember to use the correct word form.

> inhabited   constantly   atmosphere   universe   signal

1. Factories and cars release pollution into the Earth's _____.

2. The meeting is seen as a(n) _____ of the other side's willingness to work things out.

3. It would be very surprising if Mars were found to be _____.

4. The baby cried _____ during the flight.

5. The Hubble telescope has taken many beautiful photographs of the _____.

C Circle the correct form of each word.

1. More tests are needed to determine the (suitable/suitability) of the medicine for treating other diseases.

2. She didn't say she was unhappy, but she hinted at it (indirect/indirectly).

3. There's a (slight/slightly) difference between the number of people who signed up and the actual number of participants.

4. The main (limited/limitation) of the battery is its performance suffers in cold weather.

5. You can rotate this switch to (dim/dimming) the overhead light.

Part 2: Focus Areas

Focus on Language

Word Parts

Study the word parts in the chart. Then, read the following pairs of sentences. Circle if the second sentence is true or false.

Word Part	Meaning	Examples
under-	beneath; at the root	underpin, underwrite
-sci-	awareness	conscience, scientific
-able	having the ability	treatable, allowable

1. Ken sees Richard as an underling and has little respect for him.
   In the organization, Ken's orders come from Richard. (True / False)

2. During the operation, the patient wasn't conscious of what was happening.
   The patient was unaware of what the doctor was doing. (True / False)

3. Though some find the inventor's idea laughable, he's sure it can be done.
   There are those who believe the man's plan is ridiculous. (True / False)

Grammar   *Such as + gerund*

A common way to list examples is in gerund form (verb + ing). Using *such as* in a sentence, you can fluently list one or more examples of the subject or object.

Ex: Some things, such as eating and drinking, are not allowed in the library.

Ex: We love adventure sports such as hang gliding and cliff diving.

Rewrite each sentence using *such as* + the verb(s) in parentheses.

1. Some interests can be very expensive. (travel)

   _____

2. A number of actions can get you fired from your job. (steal, lie)

   _____

3. Tourists in Bali enjoy leisure activities. (swim, dive, shop)

   _____

Talk About It   **Discuss these questions in small groups.**

1. If you could ask an alien from another planet a question, what would it be? If you could tell the alien something, what would you say?

2. Over the last 50 years, people have accomplished many things in space. What are the most important accomplishments?

3. What direction should space exploration go in? Should we focus on going to Mars, improving the International Space Station, or doing something else?

Write About It

Question: How will the world react if we find another planet with intelligent life? Give two reasons to support your opinion. Prepare by writing notes on the lines below. The first few words of the paragraph are written to help you get started.

Opinion: _____

Reason 1: _____

Reason 2: _____

If we find another planet with intelligent life, _____

_____

_____

_____

_____

_____

_____

_____

Listening

Listen to the speech. Then, answer the following questions.

Track 15

1. (   ) What is the purpose of this speech?
   (A) To announce a new agency
   (B) To warn of an upcoming typhoon
   (C) To criticize a government program
   (D) To ask people to volunteer

2. (   ) What is suggested about previous responses to typhoons?
   (A) They were expensive.
   (B) They were proactive.
   (C) They were disorganized.
   (D) They were efficient.

3. (   ) If the TRS is activated, what will ships be required to do?
   (A) Head further out to sea
   (B) Maintain their position
   (C) Return to the harbor
   (D) Contact the task force

Reading

Choose the correct word(s) to fill in each blank.

Due to interference from the Earth's atmosphere, viewing stars from ground-based telescopes is already hard enough. For star-gazers (__1__) in cities, the situation is even more difficult. All the light from street lamps, office buildings, and houses constantly "washes out" the sky and scatters star light. In (__2__), amateur astronomers often get together in clubs to organize trips to rural areas. High-altitude locations work best, but low-lying areas can also make excellent viewing locations. Interest in astronomy clubs peaks (__3__) year or two when headline events like passing comets and meteor showers take place. At these times, groups made up of dozens of space enthusiasts form to explore the universe together.

1. (   ) (A) they live   (B) live
          (C) to live   (D) living

2. (   ) (A) response   (B) effect
          (C) particular   (D) between

3. (   ) (A) each   (B) every
          (C) all   (D) any

Supplementary Reading - *The Darwin Mission*

 Track 16

As amazing as today's exoplanet search efforts are, future missions will be even more incredible. Among the most exciting is the Darwin mission, a system of space-based telescopes. Darwin is being built by the European Space Agency and will be launched in 2015, at the earliest. Not only are the mission's objectives impressive, but the system itself will be a superior feat of engineering.

Darwin will study 1,000 stars as it searches for other worlds. To learn about the planets' atmospheres, Darwin will collect light in mid-infrared wavelengths. It's a bit of space-based detective work. On Earth, we know that plants release oxygen into the atmosphere, while animals release

gases like methane. These gases absorb specific wavelengths of infrared light. Therefore, by analyzing the infrared light from another planet, Darwin can determine whether it's home to alien life. In addition, the system will be the first to photograph small rocky exoplanets.

Darwin, which will be positioned beyond the moon, will have some special technical features. It will consist of four or five telescopes separately mounted on several spacecraft arranged in a precise formation. The light collected by the telescopes will be sent to a processing hub in the center of the array. Here, one of Darwin's most magical feats will take place. The reason we can't normally photograph far-off planets is because their stars are so bright. They literally outshine everything else. Darwin's central hub will be able to *cancel out* the star light it collects. That will leave only the light from the planet, which can then be studied.

Read each sentence. Circle if it is true (T) or false (F).

1. The Darwin system will be launched sometime before 2015.   T / F

2. Plants and animals release different types of gas into an atmosphere.   T / F

3. Darwin's telescopes will only photograph planets in our solar   T / F
   system.

4. The system's telescopes will be located on the moon.   T / F

5. The light from a star makes it difficult to study the planets in its   T / F
   system.

5

Crowdsourcing

One of the Internet's biggest advantages is the large number of people online. The Net is home to many companies which use this pool of users to find talent and provide services. Long-established businesses are also using the Net to find the right people to take on difficult tasks.

Pre-Reading Questions Discuss these questions in pairs.

1. What do you usually use the Internet for?

2. How does the Net make it easier to do business? Does doing business online have any disadvantages?

3. Have you ever participated in an online poll, contest, or business activity? (ex: selling things on an auction site, designing a T-shirt, etc.)

Vocabulary Warmup 🔘 Track 17

A **Listen to the unit's target vocabulary. Then, write the letter of the correct word or phrase next to each definition.**

a. attractive	f. decline	k. maintain
b. campaign	g. eager	l. more often than not
c. case by case	h. in-house	m. regardless of
d. come up with	i. innovative	n. strategy
e. consumer	j. loyalty	o. submit

___ 1. despite

___ 2. shopper

___ 3. develop; invent

___ 4. preserve

___ 5. willing and interested

___ 6. turn in; deliver

___ 7. done by company staff

___ 8. operation; movement

___ 9. go down

___ 10. commitment

B **Complete each sentence with a target word or phrase. Remember to use the correct word form.**

1. _____, when a person goes into a convenience store, he or she buys something.

2. Our _____ is to expand into Central America and then move into South America.

3. The _____ coffee maker, which has several unique features, won the appliance of the year award.

4. Generally, the firm doesn't hire inexperienced people, but they'll consider all applicants on a(n) _____ basis.

5. As she walked down the street, the _____ model received many stares.

Part 1: Reading and Vocabulary Building

1   The 21st century is seeing the gradual **decline** of traditional
business models and the rise of **innovative** new ones. Advances in
technology are driving shifts in product development, marketing, and
distribution. One such recent innovation is "crowdsourcing," which
5   uses the power of the Internet to invite thousands or even millions of
people to participate in a task.

Traditionally, companies have operated with a limited number of
people, with jobs performed by **in-house** staff or outside contractors.
Thanks to the Internet, companies can reach out to anyone with the
10   necessary skills, **regardless of** his or her location. That can mean
working on everything from an ad **campaign** to a poster design to the
invention of a new product.

The most basic type of crowdsourcing involves setting up and
maintaining a website, with goods or services provided by the
15   site's members. For example, on iStockphoto, members **submit**
photographs which are placed on an easily
searchable website. When a client pays
for a photo, a percentage of the earnings
goes to iStockphoto, and a percentage goes
20   to the photographer. Many other types
of companies, including T-shirt makers
(such as Threadless), music sellers (such
as ArtistShare), and design firms (such as
Crowdspring) are using the Internet to
25   match talented people with buyers.

Many designers are discovering new business opportunities online.

Yet crowdsourcing doesn't have to make up a firm's entire business
model. It can also be used by traditional businesses on a **case by case**

---

³ drive – push; cause
³ shift – change; movement
³ marketing – advertising, selling, and improving interest in a product
⁴ distribution – shipping and delivering goods
⁶ participate – be a part of
⁸ contractor – outside person or company hired for a task
²⁶ make up – form

basis. One striking example is in corporate R&D. During a product's development cycle, companies

30 regularly come across difficult problems which could take a lot of time and money to solve in-house. However, there are millions of smart people around the world, and there's a good chance one of them can solve the problem. That's where

35 websites like InnoCentive come in. Companies such as Procter & Gamble post challenging scientific problems, and if a site member **comes up with** a solution (which happens more than 30% of the time), he or she can earn $10,000 or more.

Skillful people worldwide are taking part in crowdsourcing from home.

40 Some companies have taken crowdsourcing to another level by partnering with **consumers** in the creation of new products. In one case in Japan, instant noodle maker Acecook invited people to submit recipes for new flavors. In another, beverage giant Calpis welcomed submissions for new drinks. In both cases, which used the social networking site

45 Mixi to attract participants, the winning submissions were made into products. This brilliant type of **strategy** not only helps a firm come up with great new products, but it also builds brand **loyalty** through customer participation.

Crowdsourcing isn't for every business, but when it works, it can work

50 extremely well. Just ask L'Oréal, which paid $1,000 for a TV commercial made by a member of well-known crowdsourcer Current TV. The same spot might have cost the cosmetics giant more than $150,000 to create in-house. And that's what's so **attractive** about crowdsourcing. There are talented people all over the world **eager** to display their skills and solve

55 problems. **More often than not**, they'll do the job cheaply. Sometimes, they'll even work for free.

---

28 striking – very impressive
28 R&D – research and development
40 take something to another level – improve, enhance, or develop something
42 recipe – list of ingredients for a food or drink and instructions for making it
44 social networking site – website where people meet friends, post photos, etc.
46 brilliant – very smart
52 spot – ad
52 cosmetics – make up (ex: lipstick)

········· **Main Idea**

1. (　) What is the main idea?
     A. Crowdsourcing matches talented Web users with company needs.
     B. Only the biggest Internet companies are good at crowdsourcing.
     C. This century, crowdsourcing will replace most business models.
     D. ArtistShare is a good example of crowdsourcing at work.

········· **Detail**

2. (　) What type of product or service is sold on Threadless?
     A. Design
     B. Music
     C. Clothing
     D. Photography

········· **Vocabulary**

3. (　) In line 30, what does "come across" mean?
     A. produce   B. resolve
     C. research   D. encounter

········· **Analysis**

4. (　) What does the article imply about InnoCentive?
     A. Its members help companies save a lot of money.
     B. The fee to become a site member is $10,000 or more.
     C. More than two-thirds of all posted problems are solved.
     D. It's the only site helping firms solve R&D problems.

5. (　) Which of the following is NOT an example of crowdsourcing?
     A. A website where members work together to plan parties
     B. An online contest to name a new line of products
     C. A website design created by a firm's in-house staff
     D. An Internet-based service matching musicians with clients

Short Answers   Answer each question based on the article.

1. How are earnings on iStockphoto divided up?

_____

2. Where did Acebook and Calpis find participants for their contests?

_____

3. For L'Oréal, what was the advantage of going through CurrentTV?

_____

Vocabulary Building

A **Choose the answer that means the same as the word or phrase in italics.**

1. *More often than not*, dark clouds in the sky mean rain is on the way.
   A. Usually   B. Doubtfully   C. Hopefully

2. If the population *declines* any further, the town will have trouble keeping its police force.
   A. complains   B. decreases   C. relocates

3. For this line of handbags, most *consumers* are women between the ages of 30 and 45.
   A. purchasers   B. targets   C. producers

4. For an army to succeed, its leader must have the full *loyalty* of the soldiers.
   A. authority   B. strength   C. faithfulness

5. Thousands of people lined up outside the store during the "buy one, get one free" *campaign*.
   A. discount   B. promotion   C. maintenance

B **Complete each sentence with the best word or phrase. Remember to use the correct word form.**

in-house	attractive	regardless of	strategy	case by case

1. _____ the weather, the race will be held tomorrow.

2. Having work done _____ is often more expensive than hiring an outside contractor.

3. Nearly every major company uses the Internet as part of its marketing _____.

4. After the samples come in, we'll decide, _____, which clothing brands to carry.

5. _____ packaging can really help improve sales.

C **Circle the correct form of each word.**

1. To encourage (innovative/innovation), we give bonuses to employees whose ideas are made into products.

2. By (maintain/maintaining) her excellent scores, Paula won a scholarship.

3. The competition is an opportunity for researchers to (submit/submission) proposals with a chance to win a development grant.

4. I know you're (eager/eagerness) to buy a house, but this isn't the best time.

5. We need to (come/coming) up with a way to win without our star player.

Part 2: Focus Areas

Focus on Language

Word Parts

Study the word parts in the chart. Then, read the following pairs of sentences. Circle if the second sentence is true or false.

Word Part	Meaning	Examples
in-	make part of	include, involve
-ven(t)-	come; be from	venture, revenue
-ant	person; group	applicant, inhabitant

1. Next year, the neighborhood will be incorporated into the city.
   The neighborhood will become part of the city. (True / False)

2. Thousands of model train hobbyists gather for the annual convention.
   It's a yearly opportunity for people with the same hobby to meet up. (True / False)

3. Reporters surrounded the defendant in the high-profile case.
   The person was ignored by the press. (True / False)

Grammar   *Present Perfect*

This tense has several uses: 1) To mention a past event without saying when it happened; 2) To show the repetition of an event; 3) To express the duration of a continuing event.

Structure: **subject + has / have + past participle**

Ex: We have already finished cleaning the storeroom.

Ex: She has taken the TOEIC five times.

Answer each question using the information in parentheses.

1. Has Mr. Grayson returned from his trip to Vietnam? (Answer: No)

   _____

2. How many times have you been to India? (Answer: Three times)

   _____

3. How long has she lived in the neighborhood? (Answer: Six years)

   _____

Discuss these questions in small groups.

1. Of the examples of crowdsourcing mentioned in the article, which would you most prefer to take part in?

2. With so many companies using the Net to get tasks done, it's possible that they will maintain smaller and smaller in-house staffs. Is this a positive or negative trend? Why?

3. Besides crowdsourcing, how else is the Internet changing the way we communicate and get things done?

Write About It

Question: Will the day come when "walk in" shops disappear and all business is done online? Give two reasons to support your opinion. Prepare by writing notes on the lines below. The first few words of the paragraph are written to help you get started.

Opinion: _____

Reason 1: _____

Reason 2: _____

In the future, _____

_____

_____

_____

_____

_____

_____

_____

_____

_____

Listening

Track 19

Listen to the conversation. Then, answer the following questions.

1. (   ) How does the woman feel about Greg's departure?
    (A) She's relieved.   (B) She's indifferent.
    (C) She's surprised.   (D) She's jealous.

2. (   ) Why does the man think Greg left the company?
    (A) To accept a higher position
    (B) In order to start his own marketing firm
    (C) Because of a disagreement with the owner
    (D) Due to his heavy work load

3. (   ) What does the man offer to do?
    (A) Assist the woman   (B) Transfer the campaign to Greg
    (C) Talk to the boss   (D) Extend the deadline one month

Reading   **Read the advertisement. Then, answer the following questions.**

Creative Consultants

Have you got a great idea for a new business but aren't quite sure where to begin? It can certainly be a complex process. Here at Creative Consultants, we can turn your idea for a pet store into an actual shop. If you're looking to establish an online business, retail store, or something in the service sector, we can also assist you with that. Our team of experts is familiar with every step of the process, from drafting a business plan to applying for a license. We also have in-house designers who can create advertisements, logos, and even websites. Once you're ready to start making money, our marketing group will help you come up with a solid strategy for reaching customers.

1. (   ) Who is this advertisement intended for?
    (A) People who own a company
    (B) People who have recently retired
    (C) People who want to start a business
    (D) People who are out of work

2. (   ) What is implied about the business development process?
    (A) It's best handled by experts.   (B) Having a website is essential.
    (C) It isn't very complicated.   (D) Shops are the easiest to set up.

3. (   ) What is NOT provided by Creative Consultants?
    (A) A guarantee of success   (B) Ideas for finding customers
    (C) Assistance with design work   (D) Help acquiring a license

Supplementary Reading - *The Netflix Prize*

 Track 20

Online contests, in addition to generating publicity, can also serve a practical purpose. One of the most talked-about competitions in recent years was the Netflix Prize. Netflix, a US firm that rents DVDs to its millions of members, recommends films based on members' rental histories. The firm needed a way to improve this system, so it set up a contest – the Netflix Prize. The goal: to create an algorithm improving the current system by at least 10%. The prize: an impressive $1 million.

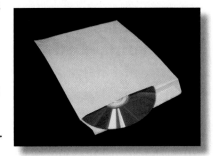

After the contest was announced in 2006, thousands of people made an effort to claim the prize. Participants included mathematicians, IT specialists, and other brilliant professionals. Though some neared the goal – coming as close as 8 or 9% – the 10% mark seemed out of reach. Over time, participants engaged in their own form of crowdsourcing and started joining forces. Finally, on June 26, 2009, one of these teams submitted an algorithm with an improvement mark of 10.05%.

According to contest rules, once the 10% mark was reached, other teams had 30 days to beat it. And one did, delivering an algorithm boasting a 10.10% improvement rate. After reviewing both teams' submissions, Netflix announced the winner on September 21. All told, 40,000 teams from nearly 200 countries had participated in the race for the Netflix Prize. The company was very happy with the winning algorithm, not to mention the free advertising. In fact, on the same day the winner was announced, Netflix released details of a new contest – the Netflix Prize 2.

Read each sentence. Circle if it is true (T) or false (F).

1. The race for the Netflix Prize started on June 26, 2009.   T / F
2. Participants in the contest came from almost 200 countries.   T / F
3. Only one team managed to improve the algorithm by 10%.   T / F
4. For the competition, Netflix spent $1 million on advertising.   T / F
5. Netflix was satisfied with the way the contest turned out.   T / F

6 Identity

Architecture and Identity

Architecture is a key component of urban identity. Buildings, and especially landmarks, are important for more than their functional uses. They represent cities, help businesses, and attract visitors. Several factors influence architecture, including local pride and cultural elements like religion.

Discuss these questions in pairs.

1. What are some famous landmarks in your country?

2. Which famous buildings in other countries would you like to visit?

3. Despite the high cost, why do so many cities want to host international events like the Olympics?

Vocabulary Warmup ⊙ Track 21

A Listen to the unit's target vocabulary. Then, write the letter of the correct word or phrase next to each definition.

a. achievement	f. imagination	k. preserve
b. contain	g. impact	l. revenue
c. eventually	h. landmark	m. stand for
d. functional	i. leap over	n. struggling
e. identity	j. masterpiece	o. symbol

___ 1. finally

___ 2. effect; influence

___ 3. having a practical use

___ 4. include

___ 5. income

___ 6. having trouble

___ 7. accomplishment

___ 8. represent

___ 9. maintain

___ 10. self; character

B Complete each sentence with a target word or phrase. Remember to use the correct word form.

1. The Museum of Modern Art houses _____ of 20th century art.

2. Popular products like the iPod can allow a company to _____ its competitors.

3. Wedding rings are _____ of marriage in many countries.

4. Whoever painted that unusual outer space scene has a good sense of _____.

5. Many city _____ are tall so they can be seen from far away.

Part 1: Reading and Vocabulary Building

1　The buildings in our lives are much more than stacks of stones and piles of bricks. The bridges we cross, homes we inhabit, and offices we work in are also expressions of our cultures. Perhaps more than any other type of structure, a city's **landmarks** are its most visible **symbols**. From towers

5　in France to statues in New York City, our landmarks **stand for** our **achievements** and shared **identities**.

Famous landmarks create powerful images that represent cities and countries. The Taj Mahal, in addition to being an architectural **masterpiece**, is India's best-known symbol. Likewise, millions of visitors

10　to Paris buy postcards featuring images of the Eiffel Tower. These cultural treasures often have a **functional** use, making them living parts of a city. The White House in Washington, DC, is still the US president's home. Every

15　day, millions cross bridges like San Francisco's Golden Gate. Even after their functional periods are over, many, like the Coliseum in Rome, are **preserved** as ties to a city's past.

Famous structures like the Eiffel Tower have been photographed countless times.

20　Buildings are also expressions of local pride. For centuries, architects have pushed upwards, starting with wood, then stone, and **eventually** steel in a race to build the highest skyscraper. New York's Empire State Building (443 meters) ruled the skies for decades, serving as a powerful icon that entered our **imaginations** through films like *King Kong*. In recent years,

25　height records have been broken at a dizzying rate, with structures like Taiwan's Taipei 101 building (508 meters) and the UAE's Burj Khalifa (828 meters) **leaping over** each other to take the top spot.

---

³ expression – something that shows how one feels
⁴ structure – building
²⁰ architect – building designer
²² skyscraper – very tall building
²³ meter – 1 meter equals 3.3 feet
²³ icon – symbol
²⁵ dizzying – very fast

Yet these landmarks are much more than measurements. They have a strong **impact** on tourism and local businesses, and they
30 can even help revitalize a city. Cities fight for the opportunity to host the Olympics, with the winner spending millions of dollars on new stadiums. In addition to becoming instant landmarks, they generate
35 huge **revenues** and publicity. Even museums can turn a city's fortunes around. After the Guggenheim Museum in Bilbao, Spain opened, it transformed the **struggling** city into a
40 major attraction.

The Taj Mahal is both an architectural masterpiece and a symbol of India.

The design, shape, and style of these buildings often evoke the spirit of the local culture. For instance, the Taipei 101 building has a powerful design patterned after traditional pagodas. Older structures like Kyoto's Golden Pavilion are beautiful examples of religious
45 architecture. Buildings can even show a city's commitment to the environment, such as the stadium built for the 2009 World Games in Kaohsiung, Taiwan. The roof, which is designed like a dragon, contains 8,844 solar panels that provide the stadium with all its energy needs.

50 Local residents and international visitors are drawn to these monuments to the human spirit. Some, like the London Eye, attract millions of visitors every year. Others, like the Notre Dame Cathedral in Paris, are timeless works of art. Whether they're 20 or 2,000 years old, made of stone or steel, or used to work or worship in, the
55 buildings in our lives **contain** the blueprints of our cultures.

---

[28] measurements – something's length, width, height, etc.
[30] revitalize – make strong and healthy again
[34] generate – create; produce
[35] publicity – attention
[36] turn something's fortunes around – greatly improve a situation
[41] evoke – bring out; remind people of something
[43] pagoda – a type of Buddhist temple
[51] monument – structure built in remembrance of something

Reading Comprehension   Choose the best answer.

.... **Main Idea**

1. (   ) What is the main idea?
   - A. The most interesting landmarks also have a functional use.
   - B. Landmarks are important symbols of our cities and cultures.
   - C. Many tourists send postcards featuring images of landmarks.
   - D. Building a landmark is all it takes to change a city's fortunes.

.... **Detail**

2. (   ) Which of these buildings was designed to be environmentally friendly?
   - A. The White House
   - B. The Empire State Building
   - C. The Notre Dame Cathedral
   - D. The 2009 World Games stadium

.... **Vocabulary**

3. (   ) In line 50, what does "drawn to" mean?
   - A. attracted to   B. representative of
   - C. responsible for   D. surprised by

.... **Analysis**

4. (   ) Why do cities preserve ancient landmarks like the Coliseum?
   - A. To carry on their functional uses
   - B. To rebuild them to look beautiful again
   - C. To model new buildings after them
   - D. To maintain a link to the city's history

5. (   ) What does the article suggest about skyscrapers?
   - A. For a century, the tallest one was 443 meters high.
   - B. Recently, they have been getting taller and taller.
   - C. All of them have appeared in movies like *King Kong*.
   - D. They will never pass the one kilometer mark.

Short Answers   Answer each question based on the article.

1. How tall is the Burj Khalifa?

   _____

2. What impact did the Guggenheim Museum have on Bilbao?

   _____

3. Why does the article mention Kyoto's Golden Pavilion?

   _____

Vocabulary Building

A **Choose the answer that means the same as the word in italics.**

1. Lower interest rates will have a strong *impact* on home sales.
   A. construction   B. influence   C. opportunity

2. Every year, third-year students *preserve* the tradition of hosting a meal for incoming classmates.
   A. maintain   B. finance   C. admit

3. The *struggling* firm went to five banks for a loan but was rejected by them all.
   A. impossible   B. financial   C. hurting

4. Getting his PhD before turning 25 was a great *achievement* for Simon.
   A. education   B. success   C. possibility

5. What's great about giving someone a flower vase is it's both beautiful and *functional*.
   A. practical   B. memorable   C. traditional

B **Complete each sentence with the best word or phrase. Remember to use the correct word form.**

masterpiece	identity	leap over	revenue	landmark

1. When stores lower prices, their _____ can still increase due to higher sales volumes.

2. The convention center, designed by a famous architect, quickly became a city _____.

3. Clothing is an important part of one's public _____.

4. A(n) _____ of writing, the novel *Huckleberry Finn* is considered an American treasure.

5. With a strong showing in the fourth round, the athlete _____ his rivals and took possession of first place.

C **Circle the correct form of each word.**

1. Here's the file (contain/containing) the patient's medical records.

2. The hospital's closure is (symbol/symbolic) of the falling population.

3. We'll sort through the boxes (eventually/eventual), but it might take a while.

4. Centuries ago in Europe, the size of a king's castle (standing/stood) for the range of his power.

5. Residents are having a hard time (imagination/imagining) what the town will be like without the old theater.

Part 2: Focus Areas

Focus on Language

Word Parts

Study the word parts in the chart. Then, read the following pairs of sentences. Circle if the second sentence is true or false.

Word Part	Meaning	Examples
ex-	outer	exclude, export
-tract-	pull; drag	distraction, contract
-wards	direction	downwards, backwards

1. Members may be expelled for breaking the club rules.
   Someone who doesn't obey the rules can be forced out. (True / False)

2. It's an abstract painting with many possible interpretations.
   The meaning of the painting is obvious. (True / False)

3. Upwards of 500,000 people participated in the demonstration.
   There may have been half a million people in attendance. (True / False)

Grammar   *Comparative Adjectives*

This structure is used to compare two things. The spelling of the adjective may or may not change, depending on how many syllables it has.
1) One-syllable adjectives **adj. + -er**   2) Two-syllable adjectives ending in "y" **adj. + -er (change the "y" to "i")**   3) Others with two or more syllables **more + adj.**
Ex: This path is steeper than the one we used last time.
Ex: Dennis is happier than most of his colleagues.

Fill in each sentence with the correct form of the adjective in parentheses. Remember to write "more" if necessary.

1. These pears are _____ than the ones from Seaside Market. (fresh)

2. Running my own restaurant is _____ than I expected. (difficult)

3. The furniture in the boss's office is _____ than what I have. (fancy)

4. This material is _____ than what you'll find on most coats. (soft)

5. Wild animals are usually far _____ than domestic pets. (clever)

Talk About It   **Discuss these questions in small groups.**

1. What interests you the most about a building? The design? height? function?

2. When you go to a new place, do you prefer visiting its buildings (such as temples, museums, and skyscrapers), or do you prefer outdoor places like zoos and parks?

3. What symbol of your country's capital is likely to appear on a postcard? Is it a building? If not, what is it?

Write About It

Question: Some people in your city want to build a new sports complex. Yet the money would come from higher taxes. Do you support or oppose the plan? Give two reasons to support your opinion. Prepare by writing notes on the lines below. The first few words of the paragraph are written to help you get started.

Opinion: _____

Reason 1: _____

Reason 2: _____

Building a new sports complex is _____

_____

_____

_____

_____

_____

_____

_____

_____

Listening Listen to the announcement. Then, answer the following questions.

Track 23

1. ( ) Who is making this announcement?
   (A) A weather forecaster
   (B) A tour guide
   (C) A security guard
   (D) An airplane pilot

2. ( ) What does the speaker suggest?
   (A) They will arrive as originally scheduled.
   (B) Conditions might be poor until 3:35.
   (C) The Grand Canyon may not be visible.
   (D) She'll provide an update in 10 minutes.

3. ( ) What is the weather currently like in Las Vegas?
   (A) Warm
   (B) Clear
   (C) Snowy
   (D) Stormy

Reading Choose the correct word to fill in each blank.

The town of Westmark was founded in 1835 by Michael Warren, a gem trader in search of riches. When Mr. Warren first arrived, he built a cabin near a river. After several years of back-breaking labor, he struck it rich with an amazing find of rubies and other (__1__) gems. He then built a beautiful mansion, a masterpiece of Victorian architecture which served as the Warren family home for 100 years. The 20th century was less kind to his descendants, (__2__) moved away from Westmark, leaving the mansion to fall into disrepair. Now, the Westmark Historical Society wants to preserve both the mansion and the site of Mr. Warren's cabin. By converting (__3__) into museums, they feel the revenues from ticket sales can maintain both sites for generations.

1. ( ) (A) extinct   (B) unknown
        (C) precious   (D) abstract

2. ( ) (A) which   (B) where
        (C) whom   (D) who

3. ( ) (A) their   (B) they
        (C) them   (D) theirs

Supplementary Reading - *Frank Gehry*

 Track 24

For many landmarks, the architect's vision and style define the building's character. In fact, cities planning a new structure often go out of their way to employ famous architects, whose participation delivers immediate status to a project. One of the most celebrated architects of the last 30 years has been Frank Gehry, winner of the 1989 Pritzker Architecture Prize. The curves and shapes of his buildings are immediately recognizable, and the structures he designs are popular attractions.

Gehry was born in 1929 in Toronto, Canada. In 1947 he moved to California, where he studied architecture. Gehry started his own architectural firm in 1962, but his fame quickly grew after 1979, when he redesigned his own home. The design showed Gehry's interest in unusual materials such as chain-link fence, corrugated metal, and other industrial building blocks. Gehry made his name with the use of such materials, as well as his interest in bold geometric shapes, angles, and curves. Soon, Gehry was involved in projects from the USA to Germany to the Czech Republic.

Gehry has designed a variety of structures, including homes, shops, and libraries, not to mention several museums. In 1997 his Guggenheim Museum in Bilbao opened to wide acclaim. The building, covered in titanium, instantly became one of Spain's most recognized landmarks. Another masterpiece was the Walt Disney Concert Hall, which opened in 2003. Its distinctive exterior is covered with curved, smooth metal plates. At more than 80 years of age, the master is still hard at work.

Read each sentence. Circle if it is true (T) or false (F).

1. Frank Gehry opened an architectural firm after moving to the USA. T / F
2. All the buildings which Frank Gehry has designed are in Europe. T / F
3. The Walt Disney Concert Hall was Frank Gehry's first major work. T / F
4. Frank Gehry is known for designing with industrial materials. T / F
5. Frank Gehry retired when he turned 80. T / F

7 Health

Food Safety

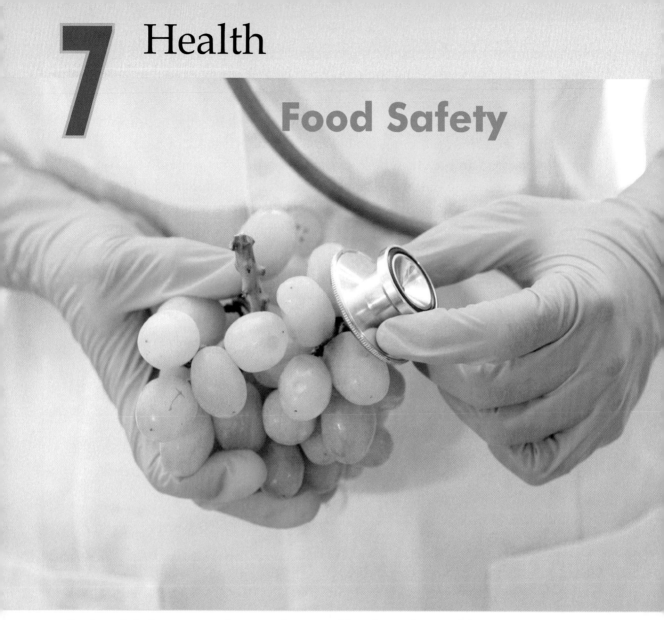

In the global economy, huge volumes of food are shipped from country to country. Recently, food safety has become an important issue. From the time it's grown to the time it reaches your refrigerator, food can be contaminated in a number of ways.

Pre-Reading Questions Discuss these questions in pairs.

1. Are you worried about the safety of your food?

2. What are some ways food can become unsafe?

3. Can you think of any food safety cases that have made news headlines?

Vocabulary Warmup Track 25

A Listen to the unit's target vocabulary. Then, write the letter of the correct word or phrase next to each definition.

a. batch	f. essential	k. occur
b. chemical	g. frustrated	l. scandal
c. come into play	h. hygiene	m. shocking
d. contaminate	i. inspection	n. state of affairs
e. enforce	j. not to mention	o. violate

___ 1. examination; close review

___ 2. group; lot

___ 3. pollute

___ 4. break; go against

___ 5. take place; happen

___ 6. bothered; angry

___ 7. cleanliness

___ 8. make sure a law or rule is carried out

___ 9. very surprising

___ 10. as well as

B Complete each sentence with a target word or phrase. Remember to use the correct word form.

1. Politicians need to be careful to avoid _____, which can cost them their jobs.

2. The competition will be held indoors, so the weather won't _____.

3. _____ are used in the production of many goods, but they must be handled carefully.

4. During the hike through the jungle, it's _____ that you do everything the guide tells you.

5. Since the departure of the CEO and several engineers, the software company has found itself in a difficult _____.

Part 1: Reading and Vocabulary Building

1　Besides being a necessity of life, food is one of our greatest pleasures. Yet in recent years, **shocking** cases of food-borne illnesses have grabbed news headlines. It's a widespread problem, leading to 76 million people being sickened and 5,000 killed in the USA alone every year. The issues

5　involved are complicated by the globalization of the food industry, as it's taking longer and longer for food to reach people. With the worsening **state of affairs**, people and governments are fighting back to make food safer.

Bacteria are often to blame, since they can **contaminate** meat, dairy

10　products, and produce at many points along the supply chain. Salmonella is a common bacterium that causes food poisoning, and a contaminated **batch** of food can sicken many people. In 2009,

15　700 people in the USA were sickened by peanuts containing salmonella. The problem **occurred** at the processing plant, which was found to **violate** **hygiene** laws. In another case that year,

From the farm to the factory to your home, food often travels long and far.

20　66 illnesses were caused by E. coli, a bacterium which made its way into cookie dough. Both cases led to huge product recalls.

Food can also be corrupted by **chemicals** added to processed food and medicine. A series of **scandals** have rocked China in recent years, damaging the "Made in China" label and causing a worldwide uproar.

25　In 2006, more than 100 people in Panama were killed by cough syrup from China containing the toxin diethylene glycol. The following year, thousands of pets died from Chinese-made food containing the chemical

---

² food-borne – carried or spread by food
⁵ globalization – the process by which the world is becoming more and more connected
⁹ bacteria – very small organisms which are invisible to the human eye
²² corrupted – damaged; contaminated
²³ rocked – hit; shaken
²⁴ uproar – angry reaction
²⁶ toxin – poison

melamine. Again, in 2008, milk powder was mixed with melamine, tragically sickening some 300,000 babies and killing six. According to reports, suppliers in China added the toxin to the products to save money or cheat on **inspection** tests.

The Chinese government responded swiftly and strongly to the incidents. Then, in 2009, it passed the Food Safety Law, increasing factory inspections and strengthening enforcement. The same year in the USA, the Obama administration started taking steps to reduce outbreaks of salmonella poisoning and contamination from other types of bacteria. Critics charge that despite the good intentions behind these efforts, they're difficult to **enforce** given the size of the food processing industry.

Washing fruit thoroughly is an important part of good food hygiene.

Although consumers are **frustrated**, they're not powerless, as steps can be taken to reduce the risk of food-borne illnesses. Experts recommend washing your hands for 20 seconds before preparing food to eat. Also, rinse produce thoroughly before cooking it. Meat, fish, and dairy products should be cooked at a sufficiently high heat to kill bacteria. Finally, when refrigerating food, make sure to separate produce from meat products.

Steps like these can help, but they don't **come into play** if you're at a restaurant or eating something from a package. Nor do they address issues like the use of pesticides on farms or growth hormones in animal feed, **not to mention** the need to make food labels clearer. For the many issues related to food safety, both strong and well-enforced laws, as well as producer and consumer education, are **essential** tools in the fight.

---

[32] swiftly – quickly
[36] administration – organization; government
[46] produce – fruits and vegetables
[47] sufficiently – done enough
[51] address – meet; take into consideration

.... **Main Idea**

1. ( ) What is the main idea?
   A. There's little we can do to reduce the risk of food-borne illnesses.
   B. The food industry is more globalized than ever.
   C. Efforts are underway to keep food safe, but it's a complex issue.
   D. Bacteria often contaminate the food supply.

.... **Detail**

2. ( ) In what year were 66 people sickened from E. coli in cookie dough?
   A. 2006
   B. 2007
   C. 2008
   D. 2009

.... **Vocabulary**

3. ( ) In line 29, what does "tragically" mean?
   A. widely   B. sadly
   C. quickly   D. illegally

.... **Analysis**

4. ( ) Why was melamine added to milk powder in China?
   A. To make the shipments lighter
   B. To fool milk powder inspectors
   C. To hurt the "Made in China" label
   D. To meet health and safety standards

5. ( ) Why is there doubt that Obama's reforms will change the food industry?
   A. There isn't enough public support for his efforts.
   B. People don't believe the reforms are well meaning.
   C. Because it's so large, the industry is hard to manage.
   D. Critics aren't concerned about salmonella poisoning.

Short Answers Answer each question based on the article.

1. What did China's 2009 Food Safety Law do?

   _____

2. How long should people wash their hands before preparing food for a meal?

   _____

3. According to the article, what tools are key in the effort to make food safer?

   _____

Vocabulary Building

A Choose the answer that means the same as the word or phrase in italics.

1. Because the *batch* of toys did not pass the quality control test, it was rejected.
   A. frame   B. tone   C. lot

2. The police officer said playing loud music after midnight *violates* noise laws.
   A. disobeys   B. complains   C. punishes

3. If your *state of affairs* is that bad, you should give up your sports car.
   A. location   B. application   C. situation

4. Waste from the broken pipe poured into the lake, *contaminating* the water.
   A. flooding   B. dirtying   C. surrounding

5. After the train broke down, passengers were *frustrated* at having to wait two hours before they started moving again.
   A. injured   B. upset   C. confused

B Complete each sentence with the best word or phrase. Remember to use the correct word form.

not to mention	scandal	hygiene	chemical	come into play

1. The deadline is next month, so I don't think time will _____ as a factor.

2. Washing your hands before every meal is one way to maintain good _____.

3. When $1,000,000 went missing from the account, it turned into a huge _____.

4. Two _____ are added to the plastic to make it stronger.

5. Driving with your headlights off is unsafe, _____ illegal.

C Circle the correct form of each word.

1. Without proper (enforce/enforcement), a law may not be effective.

2. I understand your (frustration/frustrated) at feeling powerless at work.

3. Several (inspecting/inspections) of the restaurant's cooking oil showed it wasn't being changed often enough.

4. After the third (occurrence/occurs) of the power issue, the computer was sent away to be repaired.

5. Don't worry, bringing a gift to the party isn't (essential/essentially).

Part 2: Focus Areas

Focus on Language

Word Parts

Study the word parts in the chart. Then, read the following pairs of sentences. Circle if the second sentence is true or false.

Word Part	Meaning	Examples
con-	together; with	concede, connect
-plic-	fold	implicate, replicate
-ment	result; means	argument, achievement

1. The two scholars did not concur on the meaning of the ancient text.
   They had the same idea about the material. (True / False)

2. After five tries, we successfully duplicated the experiment.
   It was possible to achieve the same results a second time. (True / False)

3. An arrangement has been reached that both sides can live with.
   They have arrived at a resolution to their case. (True / False)

Grammar   *Despite & In spite of*

Despite and *in spite of* are prepositions used to describe how something exists or happens regardless of another factor. Both are followed by an object. The prepositional phrases they form may appear at the beginning or end of a sentence.

Ex: Despite his promises, I don't believe he'll repay the money.

Ex: We're going for a walk in spite of the bad weather.

Combine the two sentences using the preposition in parentheses.

1. The new highway will be built. There are protests against it. (in spite of)

   _____

2. He is confident about finding work. The jobless rate is high. (despite)

   _____

3. The price was high. He still bought a new computer. (Despite)

   _____

Talk About It **Discuss these questions in small groups.**

1. What steps can be taken to make sure food is kept safe from the time it leaves the farm or factory to the time it reaches your home?

2. What should be done to companies which are found guilty of violating food safety laws?

3. More people are growing their own food in small home gardens. Is that something you'd like to try? Why or why not?

Write About It

Question: Do we rely too much on other countries for our food supply? Would the situation be better if there were a ban on importing food? Give two reasons to support your opinion. Prepare by writing notes on the lines below. The first few words of the paragraph are written to help you get started.

Opinion: _____

Reason 1: _____

Reason 2: _____

Placing a ban on importing food _____

_____

_____

_____

_____

_____

_____

_____

_____

Listening Listen to the conversation. Then, answer the following questions.

Track 27

1. (   ) What are the people mainly discussing?
   - (A) Supply problems
   - (B) An upcoming inspection
   - (C) The staff schedule
   - (D) Planned decorations

2. (   ) How much time do they have left to prepare?
   - (A) One day
   - (B) One week
   - (C) One month
   - (D) One year

3. (   ) When will the supplies be delivered?
   - (A) The end of April
   - (B) Early April
   - (C) April 15
   - (D) After April

Reading Read the article. Then, answer the following questions.

Last night, people living near Fairwoods Creek complained of a strange smell coming from the water. Authorities discovered a light green chemical floating on the surface. They haven't determined its origin yet, but several upstream factories are possible sources. Either that, or the chemical may have been dumped into the stream before floating down to the community of Fairwoods. Officials are advising people to refrain from fishing or swimming in the creek, as the contaminated water could be toxic. The recently elected mayor of Fairwoods, accompanied by the police chief at a press conference, issued a strong message to whoever is responsible. Besides violating anti-dumping laws, the substance may pose a health threat to Fairwoods' citizens and wildlife.

1. (   ) What is the article mainly about?
   - (A) A recent election
   - (B) A factory closure
   - (C) An industrial accident
   - (D) A polluted stream

2. (   ) What can be inferred about the chemical?
   - (A) It's definitely toxic.
   - (B) It was dumped by a Fairwoods resident.
   - (C) It smells like the area around a factory.
   - (D) Its origin is unknown.

3. (   ) The word "substance" in line 11 is closest in meaning to
   - (A) material
   - (B) crime
   - (C) incident
   - (D) punishment

Supplementary Reading - *Community Gardens* Track 28

One way people are responding to food safety concerns is by growing their own food. However, not everyone lives on property with enough space for a private plot. One solution is community gardens, which have become popular worldwide, numbering 18,000 in North America alone. In addition to providing low-cost, delicious food, these public spaces offer cities a range of other benefits.

Community gardens are located in a town or city and tended by local residents. Often, the land is on a vacant lot owned by the city. The site is divided into manageable plots, which may be tended by individuals or by the garden's members collectively. Since the land is usually publicly owned, the cost for gardeners to lease it is minimal. In fact, New York City, which is home to more than 750 community gardens tended by more than 20,000 members, charges people just $1 a year to lease a plot. Other costs involve soil, tools, seeds, fencing, and so on. However, because they're shared by many people, individual gardeners pay very little.

A community garden can quickly pay off, in terms of delicious fruits and vegetables, in addition to beautiful flowers. Excess produce can be sold for a profit at farmers markets. But a garden's benefits don't stop there. They also beautify cities, foster strong relationships among residents, and lower an area's crime rate. Award-winning spaces like London's Culpeper Community Garden even attract tourists. Beautiful and affordable, community gardens are often described as oases in crowded cities.

Read each sentence. Circle if it is true (T) or false (F).

1. There are about 18,000 community gardens around the world.   T / F

2. Expenses such as tool and seed costs are usually paid by the city.   T / F

3. Community gardens may be used to grow fruits, vegetables, and   T / F
   flowers.

4. Community gardens can make neighborhoods safer.   T / F

5. Visitors to London enjoy spending time at the Culpeper Community   T / F
   Garden.

8 Entertainment

Spending a Fortune

Movie stars, singers, and athletes are often famous for more than their unique skills and interesting personalities. Many are also known for spending huge amounts of money. Regardless of the size of their fortunes, it's surprisingly easy for celebrities to lose it all in a short period of time.

Pre-Reading Questions Discuss these questions in pairs.

1. What do celebrities, such as singers and athletes, spend a lot of money on?
2. Can you think of any celebrities who are famous for their spending habits?
3. Does money change people, or do people stay the same after coming into a fortune?

72

Vocabulary Warmup Track 29

A Listen to the unit's target vocabulary. Then, write the letter of the correct word or phrase next to each definition.

a. beyond one's means	f. file for bankruptcy	k. reckless
b. burn through	g. legend	l. roughly
c. cautious	h. lifestyle	m. survey
d. enormous	i. mortgage	n. upkeep
e. fall into a habit	j. obliged	o. wind up

___ 1. poll

___ 2. more than one can afford

___ 3. property loan

___ 4. very big

___ 5. become used to doing something

___ 6. approximately

___ 7. officially declare oneself moneyless

___ 8. required

___ 9. careless

___ 10. maintenance

B Complete each sentence with a target word or phrase. Remember to use the correct word form.

1. After years of touring in a band, the guitar player wants to retire to the countryside and lead a quiet _____.

2. To avoid being cheated when shopping online, it's a good idea to be extra _____ before making a purchase.

3. During our vacation, we _____ all our money in five days!

4. IBM is a(n) _____ in the computing world.

5. If the airline keeps losing passengers, it's going to _____ in serious financial trouble.

Part 1: Reading and Vocabulary Building

1   Considering how much some celebrities earn, it's hard to imagine them having money problems. Yet a surprising number of singers, actors, and athletes **wind up** in financial trouble, and many even **file for bankruptcy**. Through **reckless** spending, poor money management, and

5   unwise investing, some of the world's most affluent stars **burn through** millions of dollars. Few of us will ever be that rich, but we can certainly learn from their mistakes.

   When a star is at the top of his or her fame, it's easy to assume the riches of today will last forever. Celebrities can **fall into the habit** of staying at

10   five-star hotels, eating at lavish restaurants, and buying expensive gifts. The costs can be **enormous**. For instance, boxing **legend** Mike Tyson once led a **lifestyle** that cost him $400,000 per month. At one point, the late singer Michael Jackson was spending **roughly** $8 million on yearly living expenses. Another $4 million went to the annual **upkeep** on his

15   Neverland Ranch.

   Luxury items are some of the top money drainers, as stars in the limelight often feel **obliged** to show off their wealth with exquisite jewelry, clothing, and cars. One **survey** of sports agents showed they felt that 69% of

20   their clients led extravagant lifestyles. Tyson was famous for his jewelry shopping, once spending £450,000 on a pair of diamond-coated watches and another £500,000 on a platinum piece that spelled out "Tyson."

25   Purchases like these helped force the fighter, who earned some $400 million during his career, to file for bankruptcy in 2003.

Diamonds and other jewels can put a strain on even the largest bank accounts.

---

⁵ affluent – rich
¹⁰ lavish – very fancy and costly
¹³ late – polite way to say "dead"
¹⁶ money drainer – item that makes you spend a lot of money
¹⁶ in the limelight – receiving a lot of attention
¹⁷ exquisite – outstanding; very finely made
²² £ – symbol for the British pound (the currency of the United Kingdom)
²⁴ platinum – a rare and valuable metal

Spending that much is dangerous enough when one has the cash in hand. Yet celebrities, confident that their incomes will always be
30 high, often go into debt to buy homes, cars, and boats. However, once their fame declines and their income decreases, they can have trouble repaying the money. Celebrities including Evander Holyfield (boxer), Jose Canseco (baseball player), and Aretha Franklin (singer) all had to give up their homes because they could no longer afford their
35 **mortgages**.

Aside from personal spending, stars may face pressure from friends and family members who want a piece of the wealth. Celebrities often travel with large groups of people, and it's no
40 surprise who winds up with the bill. For hip hop singer MC Hammer, it's an all-too-familiar story. When he was at the top of the charts, Hammer traveled with an entourage of 40 people and
45 burned through $500,000 every month. Eventually, he filed for bankruptcy in 1996.

Status symbols like luxury boats can land celebrities in serious debt.

Financial experts who follow celebrity spending say stars need to be **cautious** about trusting others. For celebrities, bad investment advice
50 and financial mismanagement can lead to massive losses. Experts also recommend that stars plan for the future by saving a percentage of their income, since they'll likely rely on those savings once their star power fades. Finally, stars should avoid spending **beyond their means** or getting into serious debt. Rich or poor, famous or unknown, that's great
55 advice we can all live by.

---

30 go into debt – borrow money
42 at the top of the charts – having the number-one song or CD
44 entourage – group of people who travel with someone
53 fade – greatly decrease
55 live by – follow as a general rule

Reading Comprehension — Choose the best answer.

.... **Main Idea**

1. (   ) What is the main idea?
   A. Financial planning is important for all but the wealthiest people.
   B. Celebrities feel pressured to spend a lot of money.
   C. Despite their riches, many celebrities still have serious money problems.
   D. Singers spend more than athletes and movie stars.

.... **Detail**

2. (   ) At his peak, how much were MC Hammer's monthly expenses?
   A. $400,000
   B. $450,000
   C. $500,000
   D. $4,000,000

.... **Vocabulary**

3. (   ) In line 20, what does "extravagant" mean?
   A. influential   B. appropriate
   C. indebted   D. luxurious

.... **Analysis**

4. (   ) Why are celebrities willing to go so deeply into debt?
   A. They are not worried about their incomes decreasing.
   B. They think they can sell their homes to other celebrities.
   C. They have never heard of other stars going bankrupt.
   D. They receive offers from banks for unlimited loans.

5. (   ) According to the article, what should everyone avoid?
   A. Trying too hard to get rich
   B. Spending more than they can afford
   C. Lending money to friends
   D. Taking expensive vacations abroad

Short Answers — Answer each question based on the article.

1. What kinds of luxury items are often purchased by celebrities?

_____

2. What do Jose Canseco and Aretha Franklin have in common?

_____

3. Why do experts recommend that stars save a percentage of their income?

_____

Vocabulary Building

A Choose the answer that means the same as the word or phrase in italics.

1. How are we going to get this *enormous* bookcase up the stairs?
   A. huge B. damaged C. valuable

2. *Reckless* drivers cause many traffic accidents, some of which are fatal.
   A. Expert B. Irresponsible C. Brave

3. When Jack was in college, he *fell into the habit of* going to sleep very late.
   A. made the mistake of B. encouraged others to C. became accustomed to

4. On the first day of class, Professor Nagata took a *survey* of his students' scientific interests.
   A. judgment B. breakthrough C. poll

5. Due to technical challenges with the design, the R&D department quickly *burned through* its budget.
   A. expanded B. spent C. approved

B Complete each sentence with the best word or phrase. Remember to use the correct word form.

lifestyle	mortgage	beyond one's means	upkeep	file for bankruptcy

1. Creditors hate seeing a firm _____, since it can make it hard for them to be repaid.

2. I think the actor leads a wild _____ just to get attention.

3. Standard _____ includes painting the building once a year and making sure the pipes and wiring are in good shape.

4. Credit cards make it easy for people to live _____, but eventually the money must be paid back.

5. If the couple doesn't pay their _____, the bank will take their house.

C Circle the correct form of each word.

1. Strong winds forced rescuers to exercise extreme (cautious/caution).

2. There's a statue of the (legend/legendary) singer in the Jazz Hall of Fame.

3. We have (rough/roughly) three hours before we need to be at the airport.

4. Since the team couldn't agree on a way to change the packaging, they (wind/wound) up starting over with a new design.

5. Mr. Lin helped me repair the fence, so I have an (obliged/obligation) to return the favor.

Part 2: Focus Areas

Focus on Language

Word Parts

Study the word parts in the chart. Then, read the following pairs of sentences. Circle if the second sentence is true or false.

Word Part	Meaning	Examples
per-	completely; by	perfect, persuade
-rupt-	break	interrupt, rupture
-ure	result	departure, curvature

1. The lead detective must be informed of all matters pertaining to the case. *Related evidence should only be shown to him if he isn't busy.* (True / False)

2. As the file is corrupted, reading its contents will be difficult. *The problem is that the file can't be located.* (True / False)

3. Unable to maintain her composure, she cried after hearing the message. *Some positive news was delivered to the woman.* (True / False)

Grammar   *Subject-Verb Agreement & Prepositional Phrases*

> When a sentence includes one or more prepositional phrases, it's easy to make mistakes with the verb. One trick is to cover the prepositional phrase (or phrases) with your finger. Then, check if the subject is singular or plural. Finally, write the verb accordingly.
>
> Ex: The important information about the apartments is on the website.
>
> Ex: Some of the questions asked at the meeting were difficult to answer.

Complete each sentence with the correct form of the verb in parentheses.

1. The heading at the top of the report _____ to be rewritten. (need)

2. Wildfires across the valley _____ putting homes in danger. (be)

3. The statues on both sides of the bridge _____ been there for 200 years. (have)

4. Besides witness accounts, the lawyer for the state _____ there is a lot of physical evidence. (say)

5. Economists all over the world _____ gold prices will soon recover. (feel)

Talk About It   **Discuss these questions in small groups.**

1. If you were a celebrity, what kind of lifestyle would you lead? Would you be careful with your money or spend it "like there's no tomorrow"?

2. When a celebrity spends all of his or her money, who is to blame? Only the star? Or should managers, friends, and others share the blame?

3. Lending and giving money to friends can lead to problems for stars. In general, how do you feel about lending money to friends?

Write About It

Question: Celebrities often travel with large groups of people, and the star pays for everything. Is that fair? Give two reasons to support your opinion. Prepare by writing notes on the lines below. The first few words of the paragraph are written to help you get started.

Opinion: _____

Reason 1: _____

Reason 2: _____

The way I see it, celebrities _____

_____

_____

_____

_____

_____

_____

_____

_____

Listening Listen to the report. Then, answer the following questions.

Track 31

1. (   ) What is the main topic of the report?
   (A) Rising unemployment rates
   (B) Strict lending procedures
   (C) Property market troubles
   (D) Luxury real estate investing

2. (   ) During the bubble, why weren't homeowners worried?
   (A) They mistrusted the critics.
   (B) Home values were rising.
   (C) Interest rates were fixed.
   (D) Most jobs were guaranteed.

3. (   ) What does it mean when a home is "underwater"?
   (A) The owner refuses to pay the mortgage.
   (B) The bank demands higher loan payments.
   (C) The house is worth less than the owner paid.
   (D) The property's value is under review.

Reading Choose the correct word to fill in each blank.

Virginia Jefferies will never be accused of spending a fortune, unless you consider her charitable donations. Born in 1945, Ms. Jefferies grew up in a modest family. She was taught to buy only what she needed and to be cautious about going (___1___) debt. And that's exactly how she lived. For 40 years, Ms. Jefferies taught at an elementary school, and she developed a (___2___) for leading a simple lifestyle. The only times she borrowed money were to purchase a used car and, later, a small house. What nobody knew was, every month, she was saving one-third of her paycheck. On the day Ms. Jefferies retired, she wrote a check for $250,000 to a children's hospital. This modest teacher, with one stroke of her pen, became the most (___3___) benefactor in the hospital's history.

1. (   ) (A) by   (B) for
         (C) into   (D) about

2. (   ) (A) reputation   (B) market
         (C) function   (D) signal

3. (   ) (A) generosity   (B) generously
         (C) generous   (D) generousness

Supplementary Reading - *The Music Industry*   Track 32

It's often assumed that singers and musicians in popular bands are affluent. Whether or not that's true, the artist's most important source of income may not be what people expect. When we think of a singer's income, the first thing that usually comes to mind are CD sales. Indeed, their numbers are regularly published by companies like Billboard. However, other types of revenue tend to be far more lucrative.

Though the receipt totals for a hit CD are impressive, the recording artist only receives a fraction of that sum. Royalties are between 10-25% of the CD's retail price. At first glance, that looks generous, particularly if the CD retails for $15 and sells more than 100,000 copies. However, recording contracts between artists and studios allow for substantial deductions. The artist is responsible for many costs, including packaging, recording, marketing, music video expenses, producer's fees, and more. As those costs come out of the royalties, the artist can wind up earning very little.

Other income streams, such as T-shirts and posters, deliver a higher percentage of total earnings to artists. Then there are tours, which can be incredibly lucrative. All the top 20 earners of 2008 went on tour that year. Topping the list was Madonna, who earned a total of $242 million. Singers are also exploring ways to use the Internet to boost earnings. As more people buy songs on sites like iTunes, the Net is becoming an important income source. Some artists like Prince are even recording music independently and selling it directly to fans online.

Read each sentence. Circle if it is true (T) or false (F).

1. Artist royalties may be as much as one-fourth of a CD's retail price.   T / F
2. Costs for a CD's packaging are deducted from a singer's royalties.   T / F
3. All but a few of the top 20 recording artists of 2008 went on tour that year.   T / F
4. In 2008 Madonna earned $242 million from CD sales.   T / F
5. Because of illegal downloads, singers have given up trying to earn money online.   T / F

9 Nature

Wonders of the Deep

Although most of the world is covered by water, there's still a lot we don't know about the oceans. This is especially true for the deep oceans. Ongoing explorations, aided by unmanned craft, are slowly helping us piece together the mysteries of the deep.

Pre-Reading Questions   Discuss these questions in pairs.

1. Have you ever been on a boat out on the ocean? If not, would you like to?

2. What are some famous sea creatures?

3. Why is it so difficult to explore the deepest parts of the ocean?

Vocabulary Warmup 💿 Track 33

A Listen to the unit's target vocabulary. Then, write the letter of the correct word or phrase next to each definition.

a. at one's disposal	f. enemy	k. perception
b. creature	g. fierce	l. spectacular
c. defend	h. layout	m. touch down
d. ecosystem	i. mineral	n. vast
e. emit	j. organ	o. vessel

___ 1. release; produce

___ 2. amazing

___ 3. opinion; point of view

___ 4. boat

___ 5. animal

___ 6. protect

___ 7. powerful; aggressive

___ 8. arrangement; organization

___ 9. land; set down

___ 10. available to use

B Complete each sentence with a target word or phrase. Remember to use the correct word form.

1. Online video games sometimes have worlds so _____ that it takes months or years to explore them.

2. Our lungs are the _____ responsible for breathing.

3. Digging in the valley, which may contain large _____ deposits, will begin next month.

4. Many people think cats and dogs are natural _____, but in fact they often get along when living together.

5. Tropical rainforests contain diverse _____ which include thousands of species.

Part 1: Reading and Vocabulary Building

1   In the bitter cold and total darkness, there's a quick series of movements. Two **enemies** face each other, and a fight to the death is on. The smaller creature **emits** a huge flash of light, blinding the predator which reaches out with eight deadly arms to grab its prey. Though it
5   may sound like something from a science fiction movie, these aren't two aliens locked in battle. They're among the strange and wondrous **creatures** inhabiting the deep oceans, a **vast** area we're only just beginning to understand.

     Though water covers 70% of the Earth's surface, we know very little
10   about the deep oceans. Sunlight does not reach below 300 meters, and the darkness, cold, and water pressure make the depths difficult to explore. But that hasn't stopped us from trying. In
15   1960 a specially built **vessel**, the Trieste, **touched down** 10,916 meters below the surface, deeper than anyone has ever gone. So far, we've only mapped 10% of the ocean floor. However, an ambitious

Underwater craft allow people to travel deep beneath the ocean's surface.

20   project by Google, called Google Oceans, aims to map and photograph the depths so people can explore the oceans online.

     The **layout** of the ocean floor is **spectacular**. A large percentage, called the abyssal plains, is almost completely flat. Yet there are also giant mountains, some of which break the water's surface and form
25   volcanoes. Plus, there are deep caverns, called trenches, that make the Grand Canyon look tiny. Other features, such as valleys and ridges, make the ocean floor truly amazing.

---

1   bitter – extreme
3   predator – attacker; hunter
4   prey – object or target of a hunt
6   locked in battle – fighting
23 abyssal – deep in the ocean
26 ridge – raised area

For centuries, it was believed there was little or no life at the bottom of the

30 ocean. Discoveries in the 20th century, including an important finding in 1977, changed that **perception**. That year, a robotic craft 2.5 kilometers below the surface discovered an entire **ecosystem**

35 near a hydrothermal vent. **Minerals** and hot water from beneath the Earth's crust shoot up through these vents. Deep-sea

In the ocean's darkness, some plants and animals create their own light.

bacteria use the sulfur from the stream as an energy source, serving as the basis of a food chain for ecosystems that include giant clams and tube

40 worms.

Then there are the marvelous creatures of the deep which have long captured our imaginations. Perhaps the best known is the giant squid, a **fierce**, fast-moving predator with suction cups on its arms. Able to grow to 18 meters long, it's one of the world's largest creatures. Yet even this

45 beast is not the king of the sea. Sperm whales dive 1,000 meters or deeper to feed on the squid. The dark sea also houses fish with special **organs** (called photophores) which produce light. These "bioluminescent" creatures use their lights to find prey, **defend** themselves, and communicate. One creature, the dragonfish, even has two different

50 colored lights – red and blue – **at its disposal**!

Given how little we know about the underwater world, some scientists feel we should focus on researching the oceans before branching out into space. Others are interested in the economic potential of hydrothermal vents, whose mineral contents include gold and copper. Others just want

55 to explore the last place on Earth that is a true mystery.

---

33 craft – vehicle
33 kilometer – 1 kilometer equals 0.62 miles
35 hydrothermal vent – opening on the ocean's floor where hot gases pour out
36 crust – rocky outer layer of the Earth
39 food chain – series of organisms (from small to large) that feed on each other
41 marvelous – incredible; fantastic
43 suction cup – sticky area used to grab and hold onto something
47 bioluminescent – naturally producing one's own light

Choose the best answer.

.... **Main Idea**

1. (   ) What is the main idea?
   A. Though the ocean depths are largely unexplored, they're rich with life.
   B. Google will make it possible for everyone to view ocean maps.
   C. Because of the size of the world's oceans, researching them is costly.
   D. The sperm whale is at the top of the deep sea's food chain.

.... **Detail**

2. (   ) Which of the following is NOT a problem affecting deep-sea exploration?
   A. The temperature
   B. The lack of sunlight
   C. The water pressure
   D. The will to explore

.... **Vocabulary**

3. (   ) In line 45, what does "beast" mean?
   A. master   B. animal
   C. organ   D. prey

.... **Analysis**

4. (   ) How did the 1977 discovery change our perception of the deep oceans?
   A. It made us realize the oceans are deeper than we thought.
   B. It taught us that the ocean depths are far from lifeless.
   C. It helped us understand how deep sunlight can travel.
   D. It gave us new reasons to establish cities on the ocean floor.

5. (   ) Why does the article mention the Grand Canyon?
   A. To recommend a beautiful place to visit
   B. To provide a size comparison with the ocean's trenches
   C. To offer an example of an ocean ridge
   D. To suggest the sea's features are all larger than land formations

Short Answers   **Answer each question based on the article.**

1. How far down did the Trieste go?

   _____

2. Around deep-sea hydrothermal vents, what energy source do bacteria feed on?

   _____

3. What do bioluminescent life forms use their lights for?

   _____

Vocabulary Building

A **Choose the answer that means the same as the word in italics.**

1. After years of fighting, the *enemies* finally sat down to work out a truce.
   A. weapons   B. territories   C. opponents

2. If someone breaks the car window, the alarm will *emit* a high-pitched sound.
   A. shut down   B. send out   C. call for

3. Thousands of *vessels* cross the world's oceans carrying products from port to port.
   A. ships   B. cargos   C. captains

4. Monster movies feature *creatures* which are meant to terrify the audience.
   A. plots   B. scenes   C. beasts

5. The movie's effects are so *spectacular* that you can't tell what's real and what's computer generated.
   A. expensive   B. electronic   C. incredible

B **Complete each sentence with the best word or phrase. Remember to use the correct word form.**

| layout | organ | at one's disposal | mineral | ecosystem |

1. With a full production studio _____, they can put out excellent commercials.

2. The _____ of the mall is so confusing that shoppers frequently get lost.

3. The rib cage protects several of the body's _____.

4. Every animal, regardless of its size, plays a role in the _____ that it belongs to.

5. Countries with limited natural resources may need to import certain _____ from overseas.

C **Circle the correct form of each word.**

1. To appreciate the (vast/vastness) of Niagara Falls, you must see it in person.

2. The dog may bark (fierce/fiercely), but it's actually quite gentle.

3. You need to use a microscope to (perceive/perception) what's happening in the dish.

4. (Touching/Touch) down on the mountain top took expert piloting skill.

5. The (defense/defend) of the position will take all the soldiers we've got.

Part 2: Focus Areas

Focus on Language

Word Parts

Study the word parts in the chart. Then, read the following pairs of sentences. Circle if the second sentence is true or false.

Word Part	Meaning	Examples
be-	cause; provide	befriend, behold
-duc(t)-	lead; direct	conduct, reduce
-ate	make possible	liberate, nominate

1. Two setbacks, including a serious thunderstorm, befell the hikers.
   The hiking trip was free of negative experiences. (True / False)

2. Sophia, an excellent analyst, deduced the competitor's strategy with ease.
   Understanding the competition's plan was not difficult. (True / False)

3. Widening the highway will facilitate smoother traffic in both directions.
   After the work is done, there will be fewer traffic jams. (True / False)

Grammar   *Parallel Structure*

> When two or more adjectives, adverbs, etc. are in a sequence, they create a parallel structure. Words in these structures need to be the same part of speech.
>
> Ex: Wrong: The tutor is intelligent, hard working, and modesty. (All three words in the string must be adjectives.)
>
> Right: The tutor is intelligent, hard working, and modest.

Each sentence contains a mistake. Correct the error and rewrite the sentence.

1. The fans clapped, cheered, and shout the player's name.

   _____

2. I'd recommend calling Mark and tell him what happened.

   _____

3. Trust, honest, and respect are important in a relationship.

   _____

Talk About It **Discuss these questions in small groups.**

1. Some people are looking at the oceans as possible places to live. How would you like to live in an underwater city?

2. How do you feel about drilling for resources (such as oil and minerals) in the ocean? Are the benefits worth the environmental risks?

3. Movies and TV shows often focus on the dangers of the oceans, such as shark attacks and storms. Do these programs give people a negative view of the oceans? Have they affected your own viewpoint?

Write About It

Question: Should governments spend more on ocean research? Or, should exploration be led by private groups, companies, and universities? Give two reasons to support your opinion. Prepare by writing notes on the lines below. The first few words of the paragraph are written to help you get started.

Opinion: _____

Reason 1: _____

Reason 2: _____

Ocean research is best handled by _____

_____

_____

_____

_____

_____

_____

_____

_____

Listening **Listen to the conversation. Then, answer the following questions.**

Track 35

1. (　) Who is the man?
   (A) A guide (B) A tourist
   (C) A trainer (D) A nurse

2. (　) What had the woman assumed about sharks?
   (A) They are safe to swim with. (B) They are trouble makers.
   (C) They are misunderstood. (D) They are endangered.

3. (　) What does the woman think about Ralph?
   (A) He's probably afraid. (B) He's very brave.
   (C) He's well trained. (D) He's completely safe.

Reading **Read the want ad. Then, answer the following questions.**

Wanted: Research Assistant

This summer, Offshore Opportunities needs a research assistant to spend six weeks with us in the Atlantic Ocean. At our disposal, we'll have a deep-sea robotic craft with which we'll explore a newly discovered hydrothermal vent. On the research side, we'll map and photograph the vent for the Bay Institute of Oceanography. On the commercial side, we'll explore the potential of the area's mineral deposits. As an assistant on the vessel, you'll be helping with note taking, species cataloguing, and data analysis. Applicants should have at least an undergraduate degree (MA preferred) in marine biology or a related science. Ocean-based field experience is a plus. For more information, contact Rebecca Polanski at reb_polanski@offshoreopps.com.

1. (　) What does Offshore Opportunities intend to photograph?
   (A) A robotic craft (B) A newly discovered species
   (C) A research institute (D) A hydrothermal vent

2. (　) What qualification is required for all applicants?
   (A) Knowledge of deep-sea robotic craft
   (B) At least an MA in marine biology
   (C) A science-based university degree
   (D) Experience on a research vessel

3. (　) What piece of information is NOT included?
   (A) The contact person's e-mail address
   (B) The project's exact dates
   (C) The mission's general objectives
   (D) The expected job tasks

Supplementary Reading - *Shipwrecks*

 Track 36

For thousands of years, people have sailed across the oceans to trade, explore, and transport goods. However, not every ship arrives at its port of destination. Weather, war, navigation mistakes, and bad luck have caused many ships to sink to the bottom of the ocean. These shipwrecks, which are estimated to number more than three million, have long fascinated us. In addition to being historically important, they sometimes contain great riches.

Historical research is a key motivator for shipwreck hunters. Ships carrying documents and artifacts can teach us about ancient civilizations and important events. For instance, in 1977 the Pandora, which sank in 1791, was discovered off the coast of Australia. The findings from the ship helped us understand the events surrounding the famous mutiny on another ship – the Bounty. Another important discovery off the US coast in 1996 is widely believed to be the Queen Anne's Revenge, the flagship of the pirate Blackbeard.

Profit is another motive for shipwreck exploration, as companies use advanced sonar, robots, and retrieval equipment to find treasure ships. One such firm is Odyssey Marine Exploration. The company has found hundreds of ships, including, in 2007, a Spanish galleon containing 500,000 silver coins. The ship, which sank 200 years ago in the Atlantic Ocean, carried a treasure estimated to be worth $500 million. Soon after the discovery, a long legal battle over ownership rights took place between the company and the Spanish government. Cases like these are part of an ongoing debate about protecting historically important ships from treasure hunters.

Read each sentence. Circle if it is true (T) or false (F).

1. There may be more than 3,000,000 ships at the bottom of the ocean.　T / F

2. The Pandora contained clues about the Queen Anne's Revenge.　T / F

3. Modern technology is of key importance to firms like Odyssey　T / F
Marine Exploration.

4. In 2007 Odyssey Marine Exploration was bought for $500 million.　T / F

5. Everyone agrees that treasure hunters have the right to find and　T / F
claim shipwrecks.

10 Business

Product Placement

Products like cell phones and watches often appear in TV shows, movies, and even video games. This type of "product placement" is a growing form of advertising. A product placement benefits both the company placing the ad and the show the item appears in.

Pre-Reading Questions Discuss these questions in pairs.

1. Can you remember seeing any products (such as a Sony camera) in a movie or TV show? What items were they?

2. Have you ever seen a product or advertisement in a video game?

3. Why would movie makers want to use actual products in their movies?

Vocabulary Warmup Track 37

A Listen to the unit's target vocabulary. Then, write the letter of the correct word or phrase next to each definition.

a. attentive	f. debate	k. make the most of
b. barter	g. exhausted	l. opponent
c. blur the line	h. graphics	m. out of hand
d. clever	i. in order to	n. realistic
e. date back	j. integrate	o. sponsor

___ 1. make a part of

___ 2. discuss an issue

___ 3. intelligent

___ 4. carefully watching or listening

___ 5. very tired

___ 6. trade

___ 7. images; pictures

___ 8. supporter (often through money)

___ 9. believable; accurate

___ 10. start from a certain time in the past

B Complete each sentence with a target word or phrase. Remember to use the correct word form.

1. _____ learn the truth about the accident, the police need to go over the security camera's tapes.

2. Ten thousand _____ of the policy signed a letter to express their unhappiness.

3. When athletes wear company logos on their uniforms, it _____ between sports and business.

4. The train may be delayed, but we can _____ the situation by walking around town.

5. If you think her behavior is getting _____, you should tell her before she really upsets someone.

Part 1: Reading and Vocabulary Building

1   The hero sits down, **exhausted** after a long and difficult chase. Slowly, the camera pulls back, revealing his computer, desk, and a can of Coca-Cola in his hand. Movie watchers have just viewed a product placement, a process of **integrating** advertisements into movies, TV
5   shows, and other types of entertainment. The technique is a common marketing tool for companies doing everything they can to get our attention. Yet the practice is not without its critics, who want to limit or even ban its use.

Product placement in movies **dates back** more than half a century,
10   when advertisers discovered it was a great way to get an **attentive** audience to view a product. In 2007 firms spent $2.9 billion to have their cars, watches, and cell phones appear in films and
15   TV shows. Many other placements are free, as companies give studios product samples in exchange for screen time. iPod maker Apple is a master of the "**barter** system." A 2006 study found

A computer appearing in a show may very well be an advertisement.

20   that in a four-month period, there were 250 appearances of the firm's products in films and TV shows!

Product placements also benefit the shows they appear in. For small and large productions, it's an excellent source of revenue. The TV show *American Idol*, in exchange for heavily promoting its **sponsors'** goods,
25   receives $26 million from each of them. For Hollywood dramas and comedies, having well-known brands show up in offices, restaurants, and houses can make a show more **realistic**. When we see a character in

---

² reveal – show something that was previously unseen
⁸ ban – prevent; disallow
¹⁷ screen time – time spent appearing in a movie or TV show
²³ production – show
²⁴ promote – advertise; push

a TV show like *24* driving a Ford, it connects the story to the real world.

30 Capturing a sense of realism is increasingly important in the fast-growing video game market. Powerful 3D **graphics** cards already make virtual cities look a lot like the real thing. Game makers, by inserting actual 35 products, can further **blur the line** between entertainment and reality. One example of a **clever** placement is the way popular songs are played on car radios in *Grand Theft Auto*. In another game, *Crazy Taxi*, passengers 40 ask to be taken to places like Pizza Hut. For games played online, it's even possible to weave local products into a game, based on a player's location.

As people of all ages play video games, they're featuring more and more ads.

Critics say the situation is **out of hand**. We already see thousands of advertisements every day – in magazines, on the sides of buses, and on 45 websites. **In order to** preserve the artistic integrity of films and TV shows, **opponents** want a clearer line drawn between creative and commercial content. The UK took an extreme position in 2008 by banning product placements altogether.

As the **debate** rages, companies aren't slowing down. They're blurring 50 the line even further by creating products specifically for shows, like the futuristic car built by Audi for the movie *I, Robot*. In fact, all this may be just the beginning. Companies are exploring new places to advertise, including books and even songs! If there's a chance that a product placement will lead to someone buying something, it's a good bet that 55 advertisers will **make the most of** the opportunity.

---

³² virtual – unreal; computer generated
³⁶ reality – the real world
⁴⁵ integrity – honor; purity
⁴⁶ commercial – done for profit
⁴⁸ altogether – completely

Choose the best answer.

.... Main Idea

1. (   ) What is the main idea?
   A. Our range of entertainment choices is growing all the time.
   B. We see a large number of advertisements every day.
   C. *American Idol* makes a lot of money from its sponsors.
   D. Many types of entertainment work well as advertising platforms.

.... Detail

2. (   ) What firm is skilled at getting shows to advertise its products for free?
   A. Coca-Cola
   B. Apple
   C. Ford
   D. Pizza Hut

.... Vocabulary

3. (   ) In line 41, what does "weave" mean?
   A. react   B. suggest
   C. amaze   D. insert

.... Analysis

4. (   ) Why are some people opposed to product placements?
   A. They feel advertising costs are rising too quickly.
   B. They think product placements confuse viewers.
   C. They want to protect the rights of companies.
   D. They worry ads may damage a show's artistic value.

5. (   ) What does the article suggest about the future?
   A. More countries will ban product placements.
   B. The number of ads will decrease in some types of entertainment.
   C. We're likely to see even more product placements.
   D. Books will soon contain as many advertisements as movies.

Short Answers   Answer each question based on the article.

1. How much was spent on product placements in 2007?

_____

2. What are two ways video games make cities look realistic?

_____

3. Why did Audi create a futuristic car?

_____

Vocabulary Building

A Choose the answer that means the same as the word or phrase in italics.

1. The painting is so *realistic* I thought it was a photograph.
   A. lifelike   B. well regarded   C. modern

2. Since you have the day off, why not *make the most of* your time by getting the refrigerator fixed?
   A. take advantage of   B. make light of   C. look down on

3. We can continue *debating* who's to blame, or we can find a way to prevent the problem from happening again.
   A. arguing   B. assigning   C. denying

4. *In order to* save money, I'm going to start riding my bike to work.
   A. In addition to   B. On par to   C. So as to

5. When the fire got *out of hand*, the army was called in to help fight the blaze.
   A. unavoidable   B. uncontrollable   C. uncountable

B Complete each sentence with the best word or phrase. Remember to use the correct word form.

graphics	barter	clever	opponent	blur the line

1. There will certainly be a few _____ of the team's decision, but most fans will support it.

2. Cartoons featuring characters based on toys _____ between entertainment and advertising.

3. In the past, people often _____ for goods instead of paying with money.

4. The _____ for some modern video games rival the quality of what you see in movies.

5. _____ slogans like "Just do it" are easily remembered.

C Circle the correct form of each word.

1. Working all day in the hot sun is (exhausted/exhausting).

2. The (integrate/integration) of the two departments will take several months.

3. Since Mei-lin holds a night job in addition to attending college, it's sometimes hard for her to be (attentive/attention) in class.

4. Companies (sponsor/sponsoring) the Olympics to promote their brands.

5. Giving someone gifts on his or her birthday is a practice (dating/dates) back hundreds of years.

Part 2: Focus Areas

Focus on Language

Word Parts

Study the word parts in the chart. Then, read the following pairs of sentences. Circle if the second sentence is true or false.

Word Part	Meaning	Examples
bene-	good; helpful	beneficial, benevolent
-vert-	turn	invert, revert
-ive	having a certain quality	expressive, talkative

1. Thanks to a generous benefactor, the public clinic can continue operating.
   The clinic will stay open by reducing its expenses. (True / False)

2. The spare bedroom will be converted into a game room.
   The extra bedroom will remain unchanged. (True / False)

3. Informative cards next to each exhibit state the date and place it was found.
   People can learn a lot from the cards. (True / False)

Grammar   *Present and Future Conditional*

When talking about the present or future, there are two types of conditional sentences. The "real" (or "true") conditional describes what may happen given a set of conditions. The "unreal" (or "untrue") conditional describes something that is untrue.

Real: If + subject + verb (present tense), subject + will + verb

Ex: If we have time, we will visit the Tate Museum. (The visit may happen.)

Unreal: If + subject + verb (past tense), subject + would + verb

Ex: If I knew the answer, I would tell you. (The person does not know the answer.)

Complete each sentence using the conditional. The first few words are given.

1. I can't change the law because I don't have the power.
   If I had _____

2. They can't go skiing since the road to the ski resort is closed.
   If the road opens _____

3. The house is small, so we can't put in a pool table.
   If the house were larger _____

Talk About It   Discuss these questions in small groups.

1. We see a large number of ads every day. In general, do you think they work? What kinds are the most effective?

2. How do you feel about products being advertised in movies and TV shows? Does it bother you?

3. Let's say your company makes designer handbags, and you want to pay for a product placement. Would you choose a movie, TV show, video game, or something else?

Write About It

Question: Should more countries ban product placements, or should they be allowed to continue? Give two reasons to support your opinion. Prepare by writing notes on the lines below. The first few words of the paragraph are written to help you get started.

Opinion: _____

Reason 1: _____

Reason 2: _____

In general, product placements are _____

_____

_____

_____

_____

_____

_____

_____

Listening

Track
39

Listen to the announcement. Then, answer the following questions.

1. (   ) Who is this announcement targeting?
    (A) People at an anniversary party
    (B) Shoppers at a store
    (C) Buyers at a trade show
    (D) Investors at a conference

2. (   ) What is the maximum discount mentioned?
    (A) 10 percent off
    (B) 20 percent off
    (C) 25 percent off
    (D) 50 percent off

3. (   ) What advantage does the credit card provide?
    (A) A chance to receive a free item
    (B) A lower price on the day's purchases
    (C) An opportunity to win money
    (D) An option to defer payment for a year

Reading **Choose the correct word to fill in each blank.**

Motion capture technology has become a common way for movie makers to further blur the line (__1__) fantasy and reality. In the early years of digital characters in film, monsters, robots, and other creatures were beautifully designed, but their movements were not quite natural. Using motion capture, which dates back to the 1990s, a digital character can be given (__2__) movements. The technique involves placing many sensors on an actor or actress's body. When he or she raises an arm, turns, jumps, or walks, the movements are sent to a computer. The (__3__) is then mapped onto a 3D character. In the finished product, the digital character's movements appear incredibly lifelike.

1. (   ) (A) among   (B) beyond
       (C) around   (D) between

2. (   ) (A) historical   (B) orchestral
       (C) absolute   (D) realistic

3. (   ) (A) sequential   (B) sequentially
       (C) sequence   (D) sequenced

Supplementary Reading - *Opinions about Advertising* Track 40

The soaring growth of product placements is unmistakable, but an important question remains: do the ads work? When we see James Bond look at his high-end watch or cutting-edge cell phone, does that make us want to rush out and buy those products? Or does the opposite occur, with potential customers turned off by an over-saturation of ads? Research has turned up some interesting answers.

A 2008 survey asked people whether viewing product placements influenced their purchasing decisions. Coming in first place, 14.8% of respondents were likely to be influenced by grocery items, which include goods like drinks and snacks. That's consistent with the large number of soda, chocolate, and food ads in TV shows and movies. Next were  electronics, which were likely to affect 13.2% of viewers. Clothing came in third, with a mark of 11.5%. In contrast, ads for restaurants were less effective, with only 7.6% of respondents saying viewing one would make a difference in their dining decisions.

Another 2008 survey considered the potentially negative impact of various types of advertising. The poll revealed that 31% of people found ads in movies, video games, and TV shows acceptable. In contrast, 36% of respondents found such ads annoying. On the other hand, only 12% of people were bothered by newspaper ads, yet a solid 84% were upset by spam e-mail. As more branded cars, sodas, and designer bags are used in product placements, companies will need to work to keep the negatives from rising.

Read each sentence. Circle if it is true (T) or false (F).

1. About 85% of people are not influenced by product placements for grocery items.   T / F

2. In the first survey, clothing ads had the lowest rate of effectiveness.   T / F

3. In the second survey, the acceptance level for product placements was higher than the annoyance level.   T / F

4. Annoyance rates for product placements are triple the size of those for newspaper ads.   T / F

5. Since they earn so much money, companies don't need to worry about the negative impact of product placements.   T / F

White Collar Crime

Every year, many people and companies are cheated, robbed, and lied to by "white collar" criminals. Though white collar crime is non-violent, it can still ruin lives and destroy companies. Government organizations like the FBI are working hard to stop the growing trend.

Pre-Reading Questions   Discuss these questions in pairs.

1. What are some types of non-violent crimes? (ex: credit card fraud)

2. Have you, or has anybody you know, been the victim of a non-violent crime?

3. Can you think of any famous cases of white collar crime?

Vocabulary Warmup 💿 Track 41

A Listen to the unit's target vocabulary. Then, write the letter of the correct word or phrase next to each definition.

a. be wary of	f. fraud	k. recipient
b. commit	g. intended for	l. ruin
c. drive up	h. overhaul	m. severe
d. estimate	i. previously	n. sophisticated
e. executive	j. prison	o. victim

___ 1. cause to increase

___ 2. person who suffers from a crime, accident, etc.

___ 3. jail

___ 4. guess a value, time, amount, etc.

___ 5. extreme

___ 6. meant for

___ 7. in the past

___ 8. destroy

___ 9. high-level person in a company

___ 10. perform; carry out

B Complete each sentence with a target word or phrase. Remember to use the correct word form.

1. Given all the records we're generating, we need to _____ our filing system by computerizing it.

2. Naturally, when Mary received an e-mail promising to make her rich, she _____ the claim.

3. The _____ of the package must sign for it before we'll hand it over.

4. Credit card _____ is easy to carry out, since a thief only needs the card's name, number, and expiration date.

5. The _____ software can recognize a million different faces.

Part 1: Reading and Vocabulary Building

1   Not all criminals use guns and knives to **commit** crimes. Others use computers and telephones to cheat people, businesses, and governments. So-called "white collar crimes" may not be violent, but they can still **ruin** lives by robbing people of their life savings. It's a class
5   of crime which is receiving more attention as shocking cases make news headlines.

  The term covers many crimes, such as bank **fraud**, bribery, identity theft, and credit card fraud. Here's a typical white collar crime, from the case files of the FBI. In late 2004, many people received a fax that
10   looked like it was **intended for** someone else. The fax contained a stock tip, and **recipients** were fooled into thinking they had found a great investment opportunity. So they bought the stock,
15   **driving up** the price. What they didn't know is the person who sent the fax had **previously** bought shares of the stock at a low price. That person sold his shares when the price rose, earning $386,000
20   from his crimes.

Some of the biggest cases of white collar crime involve big corporations.

  When fraud is carried out at the corporate level, the effect can be even more **severe**. In one of the most serious cases, the directors of Enron, an energy company, carried out massive accounting fraud. It resulted in the company's bankruptcy in 2001, along with the financial ruin of
25   thousands of employees and investors. The case shocked the world and led to a major **overhaul** of corporate accounting laws.

---

4 life savings – money someone has saved over a period of many years
7 term – word or phrase
7 bribery – giving someone money in exchange for favors
7 identity theft – pretending to be someone else (ex: to apply for a credit card)
8 typical – common
21 carry out – commit

Who is responsible for white collar crimes? They can be carried out by an individual con artist, such as a thief who
30 steals credit card numbers. Or, there may be several people involved, which is common in telemarketing scams. Many crimes are committed by company **executives**. In fact, a study of white
35 collar crime in Switzerland found that in more than half of the cases in 2008, the criminal worked as a company manager. When fraud is carried out that way, it can be hard to detect because supervisors, expected to be trustworthy, aren't closely watched.

Heavy jail sentences are sometimes given to white collar criminals.

40 The good news is, as criminals become more **sophisticated**, so do law-enforcement agencies. They follow "paper trails" like faxes and bank statements to find out where the money came from and where it went. When caught, white collar criminals face jail time and fines, and they're often required to repay their **victims**. Yet, as many white collar criminals
45 are wealthy, they can hire top notch lawyers to help them get lighter jail sentences. That doesn't always work, though, as Bernie Madoff found. In 2009 he was found guilty of cheating investors out of billions of dollars and was sentenced to 150 years in **prison**.

Courts hope such harsh sentences will make people think twice before
50 breaking the law. Still, white collar crime continues to rise, with annual losses in the USA alone **estimated** at $300 billion. To protect yourself, the FBI encourages people to think twice before giving money or information to someone. Also, **be wary of** "get rich quick" schemes. As the saying goes, if something is too good to be true, it probably is.

29 con artist – criminal who operates by lying and cheating people
32 telemarketing – business done over the telephone
39 trustworthy – honest
41 paper trails – written records
45 top notch – excellent; superior
52 think twice – carefully consider something
53 scheme – plan; program

Reading Comprehension — Choose the best answer.

.... **Main Idea**

1. ( ) What is the main idea?
   A. Stopping white collar crime is the FBI's top priority.
   B. Credit card fraud is the most common type of white collar crime.
   C. White collar crime is both widespread and harmful.
   D. Thanks to their lawyers, white collar criminals rarely go to jail.

.... **Detail**

2. ( ) What caused a significant revision of accounting rules?
   A. The bankruptcy of Enron
   B. The arrest of Bernie Madoff
   C. The study in Switzerland
   D. The 2004 FBI fraud case

.... **Vocabulary**

3. ( ) In line 49, what does "harsh" mean?
   A. corporate   B. heavy
   C. thoughtful   D. typical

.... **Analysis**

4. ( ) How did the criminal in the 2004 FBI case make money?
   A. By selling stocks to people who received his fax
   B. By charging a service for giving out stock tips
   C. By illegally driving up the price of a company's stock
   D. By carefully investing in a range of stocks and bonds

5. ( ) Why is it difficult to uncover crimes committed by company managers?
   A. They're smarter than the average criminal.
   B. Police rarely pay attention to company executives.
   C. Firms don't closely monitor their activities.
   D. Managers commit a small percentage of corporate crimes.

Short Answers — Answer each question based on the article.

1. What are four types of white collar crimes?

_____

2. How is evidence against white collar criminals gathered?

_____

3. In the USA, what is the yearly total of losses caused by white collar crime?

_____

Vocabulary Building

A **Choose the answer that means the same as the word in italics.**

1. If you leave your bag outside, the rain is going to *ruin* it.
   A. drown   B. damage   C. misplace

2. The sign says penalties for breaking the rules will be *severe*.
   A. random   B. serious   C. expected

3. The airline *overhauled* its pricing system by setting a fixed price for every seat.
   A. abandoned   B. consulted   C. revised

4. Today's cell phones are *sophisticated* machines which can perform many tasks.
   A. advanced   B. costly   C. memorized

5. A group of *victims* of the industrial accident are suing the factory owner.
   A. promoters   B. sufferers   C. attackers

B **Complete each sentence with the best word or phrase. Remember to use the correct word form.**

prison	intended for	recipient	executive	be wary of

1. Several _____, including the vice president of operations, will be at the event.

2. High walls around the _____ are among its many security features.

3. Police say you should _____ stores that won't allow you to return goods.

4. The package was _____ me, but it was accidentally delivered to my neighbor.

5. The _____ of the award will receive a cash prize.

C **Circle the correct form of each word.**

1. The thief said (committing/committed) the crime was the only way to feed his family.

2. When we spoke (previous/previously), you said you needed an assistant.

3. With the rise of (fraud/fraudulent) activity on the Internet, many police departments are setting up cyber crime divisions.

4. Their (estimate/estimating) of the cost is based on last year's expense report.

5. The cost of oil is a major factor (driving/drive) up energy prices.

107

Part 2: Focus Areas

Focus on Language

Word Parts

Study the word parts in the chart. Then, read the following pairs of sentences. Circle if the second sentence is true or false.

Word Part	Meaning	Examples
tele-	distance	telegraph, telescope
-cour-	heart	discouraged, courageous
-ee	recipient	addressee, inductee

1. The live telecast will raise money for earthquake victims.
   Viewers will watch the program sometime after it takes place. (True / False)

2. Several hotel guests complained about not being treated courteously.
   Some people thought the hotel staff was rude. (True / False)

3. Li-wen joined the rest of the trainees in the front lobby.
   Li-wen was one of the people conducting the training session. (True / False)

Grammar   *Past Perfect*

The past perfect tense is used to describe a past event that took place before another past event. The word "already" is often used with the past perfect.

Structure: **subject + had (+ already) + past participle**

Ex: He didn't join us for lunch because he had already eaten.

Ex: By the time I reached your office, you had already left.

Combine the sentences using the past perfect. The start of each sentence is given.

1. I called to order tickets. The ticket office was closed.

   By the time _____

2. Harry saw the play before. Therefore, he didn't come with us.

   Because _____

3. She took the exam twice already. So, she was prepared for it.

   Since _____

Talk About It   Discuss these questions in small groups.

1. In general, do you feel safe in your community? How about at night?

2. How can people protect themselves from white collar crime? Is it possible to be 100% safe?

3. Besides white collar crimes, what other crimes are often reported in the newspaper?

Write About It

Question: What are three ways to stop the rise of white collar crime? Prepare by writing notes on the lines below. The first few words of the paragraph are written to help you get started.

Idea 1: _____

Idea 2: _____

Idea 3: _____

In order to stop white collar crime,
_____

_____

_____

_____

_____

_____

_____

_____

Listening

Track 43

Listen to the conversation. Then, answer the following questions.

1. (   ) Why can't the package be delivered to Mr. Martin?
 (A) He isn't in the office.   (B) He doesn't know the sender.
 (C) He didn't bring his ID.   (D) He is busy at the moment.

2. (   ) Why does the delivery company have strict rules?
 (A) To protect customers
 (B) To outperform rival companies
 (C) To meet insurance requirements
 (D) To obey the law

3. (   ) What option is not offered by the woman?
 (A) Interrupting the meeting   (B) Returning in 30 minutes
 (C) Waiting for Mr. Martin   (D) Giving her a business card

Reading   **Read the article. Then, answer the following questions.**

Inspections along Highway 65 have revealed severe cracks in five major support pillars. The road, which sees daily traffic of 300,000 vehicles, is an important corridor between Charlottesville and its suburbs. Transportation officials have closed the damaged section, and they're estimating repairs will take three to four months.

Questions have surfaced about McDougal Landworks, the firm hired by the city two years ago to conduct an inspection of the highway. Records have revealed that the firm conducted repairs on all the pillars in question. Officials are puzzled how, even with normal wear and tear, new cracks could appear so quickly. Some politicians, claiming fraud, are planning legal action against McDougal.

1. (   ) What can be inferred about Charlottesville's politicians?
 (A) Some of them work for McDougal Landworks.
 (B) They meet with transportation officials daily.
 (C) Several believe McDougal broke the law.
 (D) All of them live in Charlottesville's suburbs.

2. (   ) How long will it take to fix the columns?
 (A) Several days   (B) Several weeks
 (C) Several months   (D) Several years

3. (   ) The word "conduct" in paragraph 2, line 2, is closest in meaning to
 (A) charge   (B) estimate
 (C) perform   (D) deceive

Supplementary Reading - *Cyber Crime*

 Track 44

As more people use the Internet and more financial information is stored online, the threat of cyber crime is growing at an alarming rate. Criminals acting alone or in small groups can crash systems, disrupt networks, or steal databases of sensitive information. Individuals can suffer losses in the thousands of dollars, and companies can lose millions.

Since 2000, the Internet Crime Complaint Center (IC3) has responded to victims of cyber crimes. In its first year, the IC3 received a total of 16,838 complaints. The number exploded to 275,284 in 2008. That year, the majority of complaints (32.9%) were related to non-delivered merchandise or non-payment of money due. Following were auction fraud (25.5%) and credit/debit card fraud (9.0%).

Cyber criminals use techniques such as hacking into company networks and attacking computers via e-mail worms. In a spectacular case in 2009, a hacker was charged with infiltrating networks and stealing more than 130 million credit and debit card numbers. That followed a previous charge of stealing more than 40 million credit card numbers.

Complicating the prosecution of such cases is the fact that a cyber criminal may be located anywhere. Therefore, the FBI has set up Cyber Action Teams (CATs), which can respond to any attack within hours. In 2006, after the "Zotob" worm (designed to steal credit card numbers) was released by hackers in Turkey and Morocco, the FBI acted quickly. Within 72 hours, CATs were on their way to both countries. Their cooperation with local officials led to the rapid arrest of two suspects.

Read each sentence. Circle if it is true (T) or false (F).

1. The Internet Crime Complaint Center was set up in 2009. T / F

2. In 2008, one-third of the complaints received by the IC3 were related to auction fraud. T / F

3. Cyber criminals may target individual computers or entire networks. T / F

4. The FBI can send teams to other countries in response to cyber crimes. T / F

5. Two CATs were arrested soon after the launch of the Zotob worm. T / F

12 Social Issues

Working Disabled

There are hundreds of millions of disabled people in the world. Many lead successful careers, providing unique advantages to their employers or running their own companies. More firms are welcoming disabled workers, yet the unemployment rate for these special workers remains high.

Pre-Reading Questions — Discuss these questions in pairs.

1. Where you live, do many companies employee disabled people?

2. What problems may disabled people face working in office buildings?

3. How can technology (such as computers) help a blind or deaf person perform regular office tasks?

Vocabulary Warmup   Track 45

A **Listen to the unit's target vocabulary. Then, write the letter of the correct word or phrase next to each definition.**

a. a whole host of	f. entrepreneur	k. society
b. accessible	g. modify	l. unemployment rate
c. advantage	h. productive	m. unfounded
d. disabled	i. refuse	n. visual
e. engineer	j. reluctant	o. work ethic

___ 1. decline; reject

___ 2. without a basis in fact

___ 3. change

___ 4. related to sight

___ 5. hesitant

___ 6. benefit

___ 7. percentage of people without jobs

___ 8. many

___ 9. attitude towards one's job

___ 10. group of people living in a place

B **Complete each sentence with a target word or phrase. Remember to use the correct word form.**

1. Elizabeth says drinking coffee in the morning makes her more _____ at work.

2. To make the books _____ to everyone, let's move them to a lower shelf.

3. The _____ said the bridge collapsed due to weakened support columns.

4. Physically _____ people may have trouble working in buildings without ramps or elevators.

5. To succeed, a(n) _____ needs money, a good idea, and above all, hard work.

Part 1: Reading and Vocabulary Building

1   Vail Horton owns a multi-million dollar medical equipment company. Anthony Schwager creates and markets dozens of popular products made from his bee farm's honey. What's special about these two **entrepreneurs** is Mr. Horton has no legs, and Mr. Schwager is mentally
5   challenged. These are just two of the millions of people who **refuse** to let their disabilities stand in their way of success.

It's estimated that there are at least 650 million people around the world with a physical or mental disability. That includes an important percentage of the workforce, and the
10   number is growing as populations are aging. Despite their difficulties, many **disabled** people want to be **productive** members of **society**. They're doing university degrees in everything from
15   biology to computer science. There are also special training programs which prepare disabled people for work in offices, schools, and many other workplaces.

Lowering door handles makes it easier for people in wheelchairs to open them.

20   However, more needs to be done to welcome disabled people into the workforce. Technology is a key help. So-called "adaptive technologies" make it possible for those with **visual**, hearing, and other disabilities to handle a wide range of tasks. For instance, special software can print the contents of a computer screen in Braille so a blind person can read
25   it. Other types of software can read a screen aloud or increase the size of text. There are also keyboards designed for use with just one hand. Disabled workers welcome these advances as doors to **a whole host of**

---

⁴ mentally challenged – having a mental disability (ex: Down Syndrome)
⁶ stand in one's way – block
⁹ workforce – a country's working population
²¹ adaptive technologies – devices or software that help a disabled person work
²⁴ Braille – printed language (using raised dots) read with one's fingers

professions, from customer service jobs to positions as computer **engineers**.

30   Office spaces are also being **modified** to make them more **accessible**. Usually, only minor changes are needed, such as moving furniture, lowering desks, and installing a wheelchair ramp. In

35   many countries, the law mandates that employers make these changes if a disabled worker needs them. Firms often

Machines that print in Braille allow blind people to perform office tasks.

worry the costs will be high, but that's usually not the case. For instance, in the USA, the typical employer spends $500 or less on adjustments.

40   Nevertheless, companies are often **reluctant** to hire people with physical or mental challenges. Employers worry about disabled workers taking time off or having trouble executing their tasks. The evidence shows these concerns to be **unfounded**. However, **unemployment rates** for disabled workers remain high – up to 70% in some countries. When

45   employers do make the effort to hire disabled workers, they're usually happy with the decision. That's because disabled workers, glad to have a job, show strong loyalty to the company. They also tend to take fewer days off, and their **work ethic** is excellent.

Given the large number of disabled people worldwide, just having a

50   mentally or physically challenged person on staff can be a big **advantage**. They can help design, develop, and test products made for disabled consumers. It's a lucrative market, estimated to be worth some £80 billion per year in the UK alone. Yet we still have a long way to go to educate employers and non-disabled employees about the advantages of hiring

55   and working with disabled people.

---

[35] mandate – require; order
[38] not the case – untrue
[39] adjustment – change; adaptation
[52] lucrative – profitable

.... **Main Idea**

1. (   ) What is the main idea?
   A. Worldwide, there are some 650 million people with disabilities.
   B. Disabled workers, eager to work, offer key advantages to employers.
   C. Living with a mental or physical disability is challenging.
   D. Unemployment rates for disabled workers can reach as high as 70%.

.... **Detail**

2. (   ) What type of adaptive technology is NOT discussed in the article?
   A. Computers for use by one-handed people
   B. Software that adjusts text size
   C. Monitors designed for color blind workers
   D. Devices which can print in Braille

.... **Vocabulary**

3. (   ) In line 42, what does "executing" mean?
   A. performing   B. assigning
   C. eliminating   D. supposing

.... **Analysis**

4. (   ) What is implied about modifying offices to make them accessible?
   A. Several major changes are usually needed.
   B. It's less expensive than bosses expect.
   C. New furniture is purchased in most cases.
   D. Few countries require the modifications.

5. (   ) Why is it advantageous for companies to hire disabled workers?
   A. They will work for a lower salary.
   B. They can help make and evaluate products for disabled shoppers.
   C. They never take time off from work.
   D. They score higher on performance tests than non-disabled workers.

Short Answers   Answer each question based on the article.

1. How do training programs assist disabled people?

   _____

2. Why are employers concerned about hiring physically challenged workers?

   _____

3. How large is the market for disabled consumers in the UK?

   _____

Vocabulary Building

A **Choose the answer that means the same as the word or phrase in italics.**

1. I wonder if it's possible to *modify* the can opener so a left-handed person can use it.
   A. assume   B. alter   C. approve

2. Although the rumor was *unfounded*, it still hurt the mayor's reputation.
   A. unbroken   B. damaging   C. baseless

3. There are *a whole host of* reasons why he should go to graduate school.
   A. important   B. educational   C. numerous

4. The bank is happy to lend money to *entrepreneurs* with a solid plan.
   A. businesspeople   B. supporters   C. politicians

5. Mr. Porter is *reluctant* to accept the overseas position, since it would mean spending months away from his family.
   A. unqualified   B. hesitant   C. informed

B **Complete each sentence with the best word or phrase. Remember to use the correct word form.**

work ethic   disabled   unemployment rate   engineer   society

1. When the _____ goes up, the government comes under pressure to create jobs.

2. Laws are necessary to keep a(n) _____ safe.

3. Without a good _____, even the smartest employee is of little use to a company.

4. A mechanical _____ needs to be an expert in the materials he or she works with.

5. Mentally _____ children learn at a slower rate, so they often enroll in special classes.

C **Circle the correct form of each word.**

1. (Production/Productive) of the custom vehicle will take seven months.

2. The popular singer's (refuse/refusal) of the award shocked her fans.

3. Making the office (accessible/accessibility) to disabled workers includes keeping the corridors clear at all times.

4. I can see how living near the highway could be (advantage/advantageous) if you drive to work.

5. (Visually/Visual), the play is fantastic, but the story is a little weak.

Part 2: Focus Areas

Focus on Language

Word Parts

Study the word parts in the chart. Then, read the following pairs of sentences. Circle if the second sentence is true or false.

Word Part	Meaning	Examples
dis-	not; opposite of	disappear, disengage
-found-	basis	profound, founder
-logy	the study of	psychology, archaeology

1. Cecilia doesn't have all the facts, so you can disregard what she said.
   Cecilia's comments should be ignored. (True / False)

2. Many consider the Magna Carta to be the foundation of British law.
   The Magna Carta was important in England's legal history. (True / False)

3. The Institute of Anthropology has a new exhibit of ancient stone tools.
   People can learn about 21ˢᵗ century instruments at the institute. (True / False)

Grammar   *Reduced Adjective Clauses*

We often shorten, or "reduce," adjective clauses. If the connector word (which, that, or who) is followed by the verb "be," both the connector word and "be" are removed. Otherwise, the connector word is removed, and the verb is changed to the "v-ing" form.

Ex: Full adj. clause: This is the café which is mentioned in the guide book.
    Reduced adj. clause: This is the café mentioned in the guide book.

Ex: Full adj. clause: The people who live on the top floor are Colombian.
    Reduced adj. clause: The people living on the top floor are Colombian.

Rewrite each sentence using a reduced adjective clause.

1. Songs which get a lot of radio play can become popular.

   _____

2. Foods that are high in oil and fat are bad for you.

   _____

3. Students who plan to participate in the contest should contact Mr. Kim.

   _____

Talk About It   **Discuss these questions in small groups.**

1. Many governments require businesses to make workplaces accessible to disabled workers. Do you agree or disagree with this type of law? Why?

2. What can be done to lower unemployment rates for disabled workers?

3. If you owned a company, would you hire a worker with a disability? Why or why not?

Write About It

Question: Think about your favorite store. What can be done to make it more accessible to disabled people? List three ideas. Prepare by writing notes on the lines below. The first few words of the paragraph are written to help you get started.

Idea 1: _____

Idea 2: _____

Idea 3: _____

To make my favorite store more accessible to disabled people, _____

_____

_____

_____

_____

_____

_____

_____

Listening   **Listen to the speech. Then, answer the following questions.**

Track 47

1. (   ) What is the focus of the conference?
   (A) Disabled workers' rights
   (B) New employment opportunities
   (C) The basics of networking clubs
   (D) Workplace accessibility

2. (   ) What can people do in Simonson Hall?
   (A) Attend a lecture by Dr. Johnson
   (B) Learn about adaptive technologies
   (C) Get to know 23 experts in the field
   (D) Test out thousands of devices

3. (   ) What does the speaker assume about the audience members?
   (A) They are all disabled.
   (B) They all work in the IT industry.
   (C) They all employ disabled workers.
   (D) They are all old friends.

Reading   **Choose the correct word(s) to fill in each blank.**

Eileen Compton is an inventor who doesn't know the meaning of the word "quit." For (___1___) a decade, she has been designing vehicles for people with mobility challenges. The prolific inventor has come up with 13 car designs and two truck designs. So far, she hasn't sold any ideas to major automobile companies, but, refusing to quit, she keeps pushing ahead. To pay the bills, Ms. Compton works as an engineer on a (___2___) basis. But vehicle design is her true passion. Her latest idea is to modify an existing four-door sedan so it can be driven without the use of one or both legs. That idea, she says, may turn the heads of executives, since it's far cheaper than (___3___) a vehicle from scratch.

1. (   ) (A) near   (B) nearing
   (C) nearly   (D) nears

2. (   ) (A) case by case   (B) step by step
   (C) one by one   (D) line by line

3. (   ) (A) develop   (B) developing
   (C) to develop   (D) developed

Supplementary Reading - *Sir David Murray*

 Track 48

Though physically disabled, Sir David Murray is one of Scotland's wealthiest people. In 2008 his net worth was estimated at $1.4 billion, ranking sixth on the list. The entrepreneur has had tremendous success as a businessperson and as the owner of a sports franchise. On top of that, he has given back to the community by establishing a foundation to help others with disabilities. In recognition of his contributions to society, he was knighted by Queen Elizabeth in 2007.

Born in Ayr, Scotland in 1951, Sir David founded Murray International Metals at just 23 years of age. Tragedy struck two years later. Murray was in a terrible car accident, and both his legs had to be amputated. However, he continued pushing forward, expanding his company into other areas, including mining, venture capital, and property development.

Determined to replicate his business success in the world of sports, Murray bought Rangers Football Club in 1988. In addition to making improvements to Ibrox Stadium, he turned the team's fortunes around. Under his chairmanship, which ended in 2009, the team attracted top international talent and won nine Premier League titles in a row.

In 1996 Sir David set up the Murray Foundation. The group acts as a support center for amputees, providing services like physical rehabilitation and emotional support. The foundation also acts as a knowledge hub for amputees, distributing information pamphlets and videos. What's more, they put amputees in touch with groups coordinating recreational, sport, and other activities.

Read each sentence. Circle if it is true (T) or false (F).

1. Over time, Murray's company grew to cover several business fields.   T / F
2. Rangers won a dozen straight titles while Murray was chairman.   T / F
3. Murray was knighted before he bought Rangers Football Club.   T / F
4. One of Murray's changes to the team was relocating it.   T / F
5. The Murray Foundation offers support and services to amputees.   T / F

13 Growing and Aging

Pet Therapy

For elderly people, raising a pet or just being around animals can be a positive experience. Research has shown that "pet therapy" has both medical and emotional benefits. For those unable to raise a pet, volunteer groups visit hospitals so seniors can spend time with animals.

Pre-Reading Questions Discuss these questions in pairs.

1. Do you have any pets? What are they?

2. How can older people benefit from being around animals?

3. What kinds of animals make the best pets for elderly people?

Vocabulary Warmup 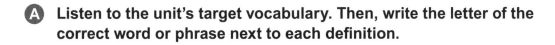 Track 49

A **Listen to the unit's target vocabulary. Then, write the letter of the correct word or phrase next to each definition.**

a. adopt	f. data	k. ideal
b. beneficial	g. depression	l. interact
c. candidate	h. device	m. phenomenon
d. companion	i. extensively	n. predictable
e. confirm	j. flexibility	o. senior citizen

___ 1. verify

___ 2. easy to anticipate or figure out

___ 3. old person

___ 4. adaptability

___ 5. friend; someone you spend time with

___ 6. helpful

___ 7. perfect

___ 8. information

___ 9. widely; thoroughly

___ 10. tool; machine

B **Complete each sentence with a target word or phrase. Remember to use the correct word form.**

1. Three planets lining up is a rare _____ which interests both professional and amateur astronomers.

2. There are three excellent _____ for the position, but only one will get the job.

3. Since the accident involving her friend's death, Janice has suffered from _____.

4. One of the best things about the Internet is the way it lets you _____ with people all over the world.

5. Mr. and Mrs. McNielsen are on a waiting list to _____ a child.

Part 1: Reading and Vocabulary Building

1   Pet owners of all ages are familiar with the joys of raising animals. For
     senior citizens, caring for a cat or dog can play an especially important
     role. Doing so has both emotional and physical advantages. In fact,
     there's so much **data confirming** the benefits of pet ownership that "pet
5   therapy" is a well-established practice. Whether seniors own a pet or
     spend limited time with an animal, they can experience a measurable
     improvement in their quality of life.

     For elderly people, **interacting** with animals has several medical
     benefits, including lower blood pressure, slower heart rate, and
10   decreased stress. The act of caring for
     a pet, including feeding, stroking, and
     walking it, involves a regular physical
     routine. That improves **flexibility**
     and blood flow through increased
15   cardiovascular activity. There are also
     emotional benefits such as lower levels
     of **depression**, decreased loneliness, and
     a stronger sense of purpose and self-
     worth.

Gentle animals bring love and friendship to elderly hospital patients.

20   If a senior citizen is unable to own an animal, volunteer organizations
     can provide pet therapy services. These groups bring cats, dogs, birds,
     and other animals to hospitals and retirement homes. Since 1986, the
     Japanese Animal Hospital Association and their cute animals have
     brought smiles to the faces of many elderly patients. Likewise, in the
25   USA, groups like Pets on Wheels ensure that even seniors who are bed-
     ridden can enjoy the comfort of a loving animal.

---

   [6] measurable – able to be shown with solid data
   [8] elderly – polite way to say "old"
   [11] stroking – gently petting
   [13] routine – regular series of activities
   [15] cardiovascular – related to the heart and blood vessels
   [18] self-worth – feeling of being important
   [22] retirement home – place where elderly people live and are cared for
   [25] bed-ridden – unable to leave one's bed

Typically, smaller dogs and cats are involved, since they're light and can fit on a senior's lap. These animals also make **ideal candidates** for seniors who want to own a pet. Experts suggest **adopting** mature animals,
30 since their behavior is well established and **predictable**. Yet there's no reason to limit one's choices to dogs or cats. Indeed, a Purdue University study showed that caring for fish was **beneficial** to Alzheimer's disease patients. Another study in Italy revealed that raising canaries led to lower levels of depression.

35 Companies have taken note of this **phenomenon** and are producing a variety of **devices** to help seniors raise animals. For example, electronic feeders release a certain amount of food at set times of the day. There are also watering machines which automatically clean the bowl and add fresh water. Mini pet walkers (basically treadmills for dogs) make sure
40 pets get enough exercise if their owners have mobility problems. Another device throws tennis balls to make it easier to play catch with a dog.

There's even a generation of robot pets being developed by companies like Sony and Matsushita Electric. Increasingly
45 lifelike, these cute robots show a range of emotions and interact **extensively** with their owners. Some, like "Robobear," have impressive functions. Equipped with voice recognition technology, when
50 Robobear hears phrases like "I am sick," it

Multi-function robot pets may be commonplace one day.

immediately contacts an emergency response center. For seniors unable to own pets or afford full-time medical care, these super-intelligent robot pets could provide a "best of both worlds" solution. Indeed, whether it barks, meows, or recharges in a wall socket, a pet can be a great
55 **companion** for a senior citizen.

---

[28] lap – area of one's legs from the waist to the knees (formed while sitting)
[33] canary – a type of song bird
[39] treadmill – exercise machine for walking or running
[46] interact – communicate; act and react to what someone does
[48] impressive – excellent
[48] equipped with – supplied with; having
[49] voice recognition – ability to understand what someone says
[54] wall socket – slot in a wall that electric devices are plugged into

Choose the best answer.

.... **Main Idea**

1. (　) What is the main idea?
   A. Spending time with an animal can greatly benefit elderly people.
   B. Pets are a joy for people of all ages.
   C. Small animals that can fit on one's lap make ideal pets for seniors.
   D. Electronic feeders are useful but expensive.

.... **Detail**

2. (　) What benefit of pet ownership is NOT discussed in the article?
   A. Improved blood circulation   B. Lower stress levels
   C. Longer life expectancy   D. Better flexibility

.... **Vocabulary**

3. (　) In line 25, what does "ensure" mean?
   A. make mention   B. make friends
   C. make clear   D. make certain

.... **Analysis**

4. (　) What do the Japanese Animal Hospital Association and Pets on Wheels have in common?
   A. They both allow seniors to be with animals.
   B. Both of them are based in Asia.
   C. The organizations were both founded in 1986.
   D. Neither of them deal with birds.

5. (　) What can be inferred about the Italian study?
   A. The study was performed by Purdue University scientists.
   B. The researchers would likely recommend that seniors raise birds.
   C. The conclusion differs from widespread attitudes about pet therapy.
   D. The depression levels of seniors were only measured once.

Short Answers **Answer each question based on the article.**

1. Why is it better for seniors to raise mature animals?

   _____

2. Why would a senior citizen need to buy a mini pet walker?

   _____

3. In what ways are robot pets similar to real animals?

   _____

Vocabulary Building

A **Choose the answer that means the same as the word in italics.**

1. This *device* lets rescuers remotely look inside a collapsed building.
   A. situation   B. officer   C. machine

2. If a friend is going through *depression*, just being there for him or her can be helpful.
   A. emotion   B. stability   C. unhappiness

3. Thousands of zebras crossing the African plains is a *phenomenon* that must be seen to be believed.
   A. location   B. species   C. happening

4. The *data* suggests movie audiences have shrunk in recent years.
   A. facts   B. entertainment   C. analysis

5. I've looked through the records *extensively*, but I can't find mention of anyone by that name.
   A. exclusively   B. thoroughly   C. secretly

B **Complete each sentence with the best word or phrase. Remember to use the correct word form.**

> flexibility   senior citizen   adopt   companion   candidate

1. Since you'll be moving once every few years, the appointment requires a degree of _____.

2. The community center is designed for _____, so there are full-time medical personnel on staff.

3. The elderly roommates have been _____ for almost 50 years.

4. Samantha plans to _____ a dog from a local animal shelter.

5. Brazil has everything we're looking for, so it's the top _____ for our next vacation.

C **Circle the correct form of each word.**

1. (Ideal/Ideally), I'd like to be on the road by 9:30.

2. As soon as we have (confirm/confirmation) that the funds are in the account, we'll ship the goods.

3. The (predictable/predictability) of the city's traffic patterns makes it easy to program the traffic lights.

4. One of the (benefits/beneficial) of living here is the abundance of restaurants.

5. The retired teacher misses (interact/interacting) with her students.

Part 2: Focus Areas

Focus on Language

Word Parts

Study the word parts in the chart. Then, read the following pairs of sentences. Circle if the second sentence is true or false.

Word Part	Meaning	Examples
pro-	forward	proceed, protect
-dict-	say	verdict, dictate
-eer	one who performs a task	engineer, mountaineer

1. The meeting was prolonged by Bob's introduction of a new issue.
   Thanks to Bob, it was possible to end the meeting early. (True / False)

2. In the story, the queen's edict is obeyed without question.
   Only a few dare challenge the queen's order. (True / False)

3. The order of items will be determined by the auctioneer.
   The person running the auction will decide the sequence. (True / False)

Grammar *So...that*

This structure is used for emphasis. It shows how one thing, because of its extreme quality, leads to something else.
Structure: **S + V + so + (adjective, adverb, or quantifier) + that + S + V**
Ex: The machine was so old that nobody knew how to use it.
Ex: He walks so quickly that I can barely keep up with him.
Ex: I ate so many carrots that my skin turned orange.

Combine the two sentences using *so...that*.

1. Irene has a lot of dogs. Her house looks like a pet store.

   _____

2. It was very cloudy last night. You couldn't see the stars.

   _____

3. Diane is laughing very loudly. Everyone is staring at her.

   _____

Talk About It   **Discuss these questions in small groups.**

1. Of the benefits of pet therapy mentioned in the article, which do you feel are the most important?

2. What problems may elderly people have raising an animal?

3. If you could design a robot pet for a senior citizen, what animal would it be? What functions would it have?

Write About It

Question: What's better for a senior citizen – raising a live animal or a robot pet? Give two reasons to support your opinion. Prepare by writing notes on the lines below. The first few words of the paragraph are written to help you get started.

Opinion: _____

Reason 1: _____

Reason 2: _____

The way I see it, the best pets for senior citizens are _____

_____

_____

_____

_____

_____

_____

_____

Listening Listen to the conversation. Then, answer the following questions.

Track 51

1. ( ) Where are the people?
   (A) At a shareholders' meeting   (B) At a job interview
   (C) At a press conference   (D) At an employee seminar

2. ( ) What does the man suggest about the paper industry?
   (A) Every firm has had difficulties.
   (B) Only United Paper will turn a profit.
   (C) Several companies will go bankrupt.
   (D) High labor costs are causing problems.

3. ( ) How much did the firm save by reducing expenses?
   (A) 25 million euros   (B) 300 million euros
   (C) 500 million euros   (D) 1 billion euros

Reading Read the announcement. Then, answer the following questions.

This Saturday (May 15) from 12:00-5:00, the Richmond County Humane Society will host an event at the Richmond Mall. The RCHS will set up a small booth in front of the west entrance. They'll bring six dogs and six cats which you and your family can choose from to adopt. The animals are all clean, healthy, and vaccinated.

In addition to the 12 furry friends, the RCHS will bring some excellent literature. The information packets will contain a wealth of information about pet nutrition and health. Also, at 2:00, Dr. Lisa Jefferson, a local veterinarian, will deliver a 30-minute lecture. She'll talk about the many benefits an animal companion can bring to senior citizens.

1. ( ) What is the purpose of this announcement?
   (A) To tell people how to donate to the RCHS
   (B) To deliver information about pet nutrition
   (C) To bring attention to the problems of seniors
   (D) To provide details about an upcoming event

2. ( ) What time will the lecture conclude?
   (A) 12:00 PM   (B) 2:00 PM
   (C) 2:30 PM   (D) 5:00 PM

3. ( ) What will NOT be brought by the RCHS?
   (A) Half a dozen dogs   (B) Pet food samples
   (C) A small table   (D) Educational materials

Supplementary Reading - *Elderly Animals*

 Track 52

Just as people age, so do our pets. Unfortunately, many senior pets are given up and placed in animal shelters. Some owners can't afford the high medical costs. Others, who are also elderly, can no longer care for them. To meet the needs of senior pets, a number of charities have been established. In addition to running workshops on caring for older animals, these non-profit organizations adopt and look after senior pets.

One such group is BrightHaven, a California-based charity. Founded more than 15 years ago, the group takes in animals which are at least 16 years old. The animals are well fed, given excellent medical care, and free to stay inside or run around outdoors. At any given time, several dozen animals can be found living at BrightHaven. Currently, that includes cats, dogs, goats, chickens, horses, geese, and even a giant pig weighing more than 770 pounds! The residents often live to a very old age. In fact, one of the cats lived to the remarkable age of 34.

SAINTS, located in British Columbia, Canada, is another pet sanctuary for senior animals. The charity owns a three-acre estate with open fields and a pond. Since its foundation in 2004, SAINTS has cared for several hundred animals. Often, they find people willing to open their homes to a senior pet. When they can't, or when the animal requires serious medical care, it lives on the estate. There, it's cared for by volunteers. Like at BrightHaven, a variety of animals live at the facility.

Read each sentence. Circle if it is true (T) or false (F).

1. The cost of treating expensive illnesses may lead to people giving up their pets.　　T / F

2. A ten-year-old cat would be welcome to live at BrightHaven.　　T / F

3. At BrightHaven, animals are always kept inside.　　T / F

4. Both the charities discussed are in North America.　　T / F

5. Besides cats and dogs, SAINTS is likely to care for other types of animals.　　T / F

Science and Technology

Quantum Computers

Today's computers may be fast, but their speed is nothing compared to what the computers of the future will clock in at. The next generation, called quantum computers, will operate in very different ways from today's systems. They'll allow us to perform tasks that we can only dream about today.

Pre-Reading Questions   Discuss these questions in pairs.

1. In terms of performance, how are today's computers different from the computers of 20 years ago?

2. What will computers be like 20 years from now?

3. Do you feel safe buying things on the Internet and sending information online? Why or why not?

Vocabulary Warmup 🔘 Track 53

A Listen to the unit's target vocabulary. Then, write the letter of the correct word or phrase next to each definition.

a. approach	f. made up of	k. simultaneous
b. artificial	g. multiple	l. superb
c. atomic	h. physics	m. theoretical
d. chip	i. practical	n. transaction
e. in the meantime	j. shrink	o. yield

___ 1. excellent

___ 2. man-made

___ 3. make smaller

___ 4. deal; exchange

___ 5. deliver; produce

___ 6. meanwhile

___ 7. more than one

___ 8. happening at the same time

___ 9. comprising; composed of

___ 10. come near

B Complete each sentence with a target word or phrase. Remember to use the correct word form.

1. The underwater breathing device isn't _____, since it's the size of a horse.

2. Without the aid of a powerful microscope, the human eye can't see what's happening at the _____ level.

3. The computer _____ in today's video game systems are more powerful than those in the first supercomputers.

4. The idea of an elevator to space is currently _____, but it may be possible to build one in the future.

5. _____ textbooks often include real-world examples to help students understand the laws of nature.

Part 1: Reading and Vocabulary Building

1   Regardless of how fast computers become, there's no such thing as "fast enough." New uses are always being found, such as the challenge of sorting through the mountains of data collected by businesses. Unfortunately, the "classical" computers we currently use are reaching

5   their technological limits. **In the meantime**, scientists are racing to create an entirely new kind of computer, built around particles at the **atomic** level. These "quantum computers" could become one of the 21st century's most important technologies.

  The heart of a computer is its CPU, a **chip** containing many transistors.

10   Over the last few decades, advances have allowed us to **shrink** transistors so millions can be placed on a single chip. But the end of this technology is **approaching**. At the current rate of

15   development, transistors will reach the size of a single atom by 2020. That's a serious problem, since particles that small do not follow the normal laws of **physics**. Indeed, an entirely new kind of

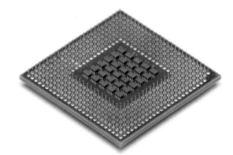

Classical CPUs are rapidly nearing their technological limits.

20   computer must be designed, based on quantum mechanics.

  Classical and quantum computers operate in very different ways. In a classical computer, transistors hold one value (0 or 1), letting them perform one operation at a time. Quantum computers, in contrast, use particles (such as atoms or ions) instead of transistors. These so-

25   called "qubits" are very special. As strange as it sounds, a qubit can be both 0 and 1 *at the same time*. This ability lets a qubit perform **multiple** operations simultaneously. A quantum computer with just a few

---

⁴ classical computer – computer using CPUs which contain many transistors
⁵ race – act as quickly as possible
⁶ particle – extremely small unit of matter, such as an atom, ion, etc.
⁹ transistor – small device used in electronics to switch or amplify a signal
²⁰ quantum mechanics – physics describing particles at the atomic level

hundred qubits could perform many **simultaneous** operations. That would
30 make the machine extremely powerful.

Cooling requirements are a serious issue for some quantum computers.

What about the feasibility of building such a system? Through most of the 20th century, a majority of work in the field was **theoretical**. Finally, in 1998
35 scientists at MIT built the first quantum computer, **made up of** just two atoms. The first eight-qubit system was built in 2005. Then, in 2009 researchers built a computer using **artificial** qubits. The goal is to create a system with several thousand qubits. Such a
40 machine would be more powerful than today's fastest supercomputers.

Quantum computers will have many **practical** uses. They'll be ideal for searching through large databases. They could also assist doctors in creating personalized medicine for a patient. It's also believed that these systems will crack the world's strongest codes, which are used to protect
45 data, Internet **transactions**, and so on. The good news is, not only are quantum computers **superb** code crackers, but they can also be used for an entirely new kind of security system. In a quantum system, the data can only be read by the sender and intended receiver.

Although the future of quantum computers is promising, major
50 challenges remain. One problem is error correction, which is harder to manage in a quantum system. There are also cooling issues, as some types of quantum computers must be kept incredibly cold. Nevertheless, businesses and governments have high hopes for the technology. Though a thousand-qubit computer may be decades away, building one is an
55 important goal which could **yield** amazing rewards.

---

31 feasibility – likelihood; possibility
33 majority – more than 50%
41 ideal – perfect
42 database – storehouse of information
53 high hopes – positive expectations

Choose the best answer.

.... Main Idea

1. (   ) What is the main idea?
   A. In the future, quantum computers will make the Internet safer.
   B. Instead of transistors, quantum computers are made up of qubits.
   C. The best research on quantum computers is being done at MIT.
   D. Quantum computers, though hard to design, have great potential.

.... Detail

2. (   ) When was the first computer containing man-made qubits built?
   A. 1998
   B. 2000
   C. 2005
   D. 2009

.... Vocabulary

3. (   ) In line 44, what does "crack" mean?
   A. break   B. measure
   C. protect   D. transport

.... Analysis

4. (   ) Why is the size of transistors becoming a problem?
   A. They are becoming too large to use with modern CPUs.
   B. At atomic sizes, current production methods can no longer be used.
   C. Only 2,020 million transistors can fit onto a single chip.
   D. Using quantum mechanics to design transistors is against the law.

5. (   ) How do qubits differ from transistors?
   A. Unlike transistors, qubits can hold multiple values at the same time.
   B. Currently, only qubits are used in computers.
   C. Qubits are many times the size of transistors.
   D. Qubits are entirely theoretical and have never been used in practice.

Short Answers   Answer each question based on the article.

1. Where was the first quantum computer built?

_____

2. What are three uses of quantum computers?

_____

3. What are two problems with building quantum computers?

_____

Vocabulary Building

A **Choose the answer that means the same as the word or phrase in italics.**

1. *Artificial* colorings are used to make the candy very bright.
   A. Superficial　　B. Manufactured　C. Introductory

2. Tests of the new battery have *yielded* excellent power and durability results.
   A. produced　　　B. sacrificed　　C. challenged

3. Every *transaction* at a bank is recorded by security cameras.
   A. interaction　　B. abstraction　　C. attraction

4. If revenues *shrink* any further, the store will have to lay off staff or close altogether.
   A. transfer　　　B. calculate　　C. contract

5. How many members is the group *made up of*?
   A. donating　　　B. containing　　C. approving

B **Complete each sentence with the best word or phrase. Remember to use the correct word form.**

practical	in the meantime	atomic	physics	chip

1. The dryer will take another 30 minutes to finish the job. _____, let's get something to drink.

2. As computer _____ become more powerful, they're able to carry out more tasks.

3. _____ energy contributes to many countries' power supplies.

4. Among other things, _____ describes the way a planet orbits a star.

5. Suggesting they walk home isn't a(n) _____ solution, since they live 20 miles away.

C **Circle the correct form of each word.**

1. Both racers crossed the finish line (simultaneous/simultaneously).

2. As you (approach/approaching) our town, the road will get steeper.

3. To win the debate, you'll need to be nothing short of (superb/superbly).

4. (Theoretical/Theoretically), many ideas are possible; however, realizing them is often time consuming and expensive.

5. In the movie, the little creatures (multiple/multiply) when water is poured on them.

Part 2: Focus Areas

Focus on Language

Word Parts

Study the word parts in the chart. Then, read the following pairs of sentences. Circle if the second sentence is true or false.

Word Part	Meaning	Examples
trans-	across	transfer, transcend
-cred-	believe	discredit, credibility
-ion	showing an action	confession, tension

1. It's easier for satellites to transmit data when the sky is clear.
   During a storm, sending data may be difficult. (True / False)

2. Frida was incredulous when she heard her favorite store was closing.
   She was expecting to hear the news about the shop. (True / False)

3. The discovery of cracks in a support pillar led to the suspension of the line.
   Service on the line was stopped after structural damage was found. (True / False)

Grammar — Noun Clauses

Noun clauses act as nouns, providing information, ideas, and so on. A noun clause can be the subject or object of a sentence.

Type 1: connecting word (that, what, where, etc.) + subject + verb
   Ex: I understand what he is trying to say.

Type 2: connecting word + verb
   Ex: Can you please tell me who delivered this package?

Combine the two sentences using the connector word in parentheses.

1. Please find something out. Who placed an order for a new desk? (who)

   _____

2. I need to know something. Where is the meeting being held? (where)

   _____

3. They are suggesting something. It is impossible to believe. (What)

   _____

Talk About It   **Discuss these questions in small groups.**

1. What will be the most important uses of quantum computers? (Use examples from the article and/or think of your own.)

2. One characteristic of modern life is the huge amount of information we deal with. Do you ever feel like it's too much to handle?

3. Some people believe technology makes people lazy by doing too much for us. Do you agree or disagree? Why?

Write About It

Question: Quantum computers will be very powerful. Is there a danger in computers becoming too powerful? Give two reasons to support your opinion. Prepare by writing notes on the lines below. The first few words of the paragraph are written to help you get started.

Opinion: _____

Reason 1: _____

Reason 2: _____

Computers that are extremely powerful will _____

_____

_____

_____

_____

_____

_____

_____

_____

Listening Listen to the recording. Then, answer the following questions.

Track 55

1. (   ) What is the purpose of this helpline?
    (A) To serve a firm's customers
    (B) To handle corporate accounts
    (C) To deal with press relations
    (D) To screen new job applicants

2. (   ) What time do stores close on Thursdays?
    (A) 9:00 PM   (B) 10:00 PM
    (C) 11:00 PM   (D) 12:00 midnight

3. (   ) What is suggested about Omega Computer's products?
    (A) They are cheapest when bought online.
    (B) They may not be available over the phone.
    (C) They are guaranteed to last for years.
    (D) They may be discounted by a salesperson.

Reading Choose the correct word to fill in each blank.

There are hundreds of millions of computers around the world, yet we only use them a fraction of the time. To make the most of idle computers, people can (___1___) them for scientific tasks. For example, using radio telescopes, the SETI project collects data from space in search of intelligent life. It's a massive amount of information, so (___2___) have asked for assistance from the general public. Each participant in "SETI@Home" downloads a program. Next, they're sent a small data packet, which their computer works on (___3___) the person wants. The network, made up of millions of machines, has already gone through a significant amount of material. They haven't yet found evidence of alien life, but this practical group effort, on a global scale, could one day yield results.

1. (   ) (A) surround   (B) volunteer
        (C) illustrate   (D) aggravate

2. (   ) (A) organizing   (B) organize
        (C) organization   (D) organizers

3. (   ) (A) whoever   (B) whatever
        (C) whenever   (D) whichever

Supplementary Reading - *Quantum Cryptography* Track 56

Besides protecting Internet transactions, cryptography (or "code making") keeps records secure, including those vital to a country's national security. For that reason, government agencies such as the CIA are investing heavily in quantum computers. On the one hand, governments want to be able to crack codes. On the other hand, they want to create safe new quantum encryption systems.

Some of today's most advanced cryptography systems deal with prime factors. A number's prime factors are the two prime numbers which, when multiplied together, give you the larger number. It's easy to figure out the prime factors of a small number like 15 (5 and 3). However, for much larger numbers, which are used for data encryption, it would take millions of years  using today's computers. But that system's usefulness may be nearing its end. Quantum computers, because they can perform simultaneous operations, are very good at figuring out prime factors. When they become powerful enough, they'll make today's encryption systems unsecure.

Quantum cryptography is so safe because of the nature of quantum mechanics. When someone (such as a thief) intercepts a transmission between two quantum computers, the simple act of looking at the transmission destroys it. Only the sender and receiver can know what's happening. Also, in a quantum system, two qubits can become connected, which is called "entanglement." When qubits in two computers are entangled, they create a perfect "lock and key" system. Again, only your computer and the computer you send information to can be involved in the data transfer.

Read each sentence. Circle if it is true (T) or false (F).

1. Governments want to prevent quantum computers from being built.   T / F
2. Cryptography uses small prime numbers to secure transactions.   T / F
3. Quantum computers may lead to the end of today's encryption systems.   T / F
4. Using a quantum computer, a thief can steal and read any transmission.   T / F
5. Entangled qubits form a securely encrypted system.   T / F

15 Globalization

Breaking the Poverty Cycle

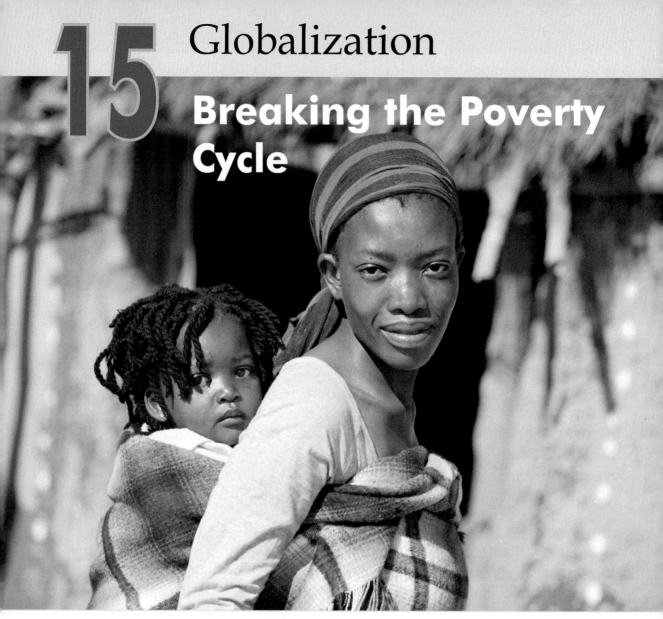

A large part of the world's population lives in poverty, which is often passed on from parents to children. Steps are being taken by governments and private groups to address the key issues. Though the problem is complex, some countries have successfully broken the poverty cycle.

Pre-Reading Questions Discuss these questions in pairs.

1. What parts of the world are home to many poor people?

2. There's so much wealth in the world. Why are some places still very poor?

3. If someone is poor, is it easy for him or her to escape poverty and live a better life? Why or why not?

Vocabulary Warmup 🔘 Track 57

A Listen to the unit's target vocabulary. Then, write the letter of the correct word or phrase next to each definition.

a. barely	f. equation	k. priority
b. burden	g. infected	l. stamp out
c. channel	h. lack	m. survive
d. community	i. nutrition	n. take for granted
e. complex	j. poverty	o. vaccine

___ 1. be without

___ 2. eliminate

___ 3. hardly

___ 4. complicated

___ 5. something that is very important; at the top of a list

___ 6. injection that prevents disease

___ 7. direct; flow

___ 8. stay alive; carry on

___ 9. responsibility; trouble

___ 10. the state of living in very poor conditions

B Complete each sentence with a target word or phrase. Remember to use the correct word form.

1. Fresh fruits and vegetables are good sources of _____.

2. Researchers studying diseases wear special equipment to keep from being _____.

3. As the math _____ is so long, few students are able to memorize it.

4. There's a(n) _____ of about 200 people living in the valley.

5. Though one's income should not be _____, many people spend money as if the supply were endless.

Part 1: Reading and Vocabulary Building

1 Food. Education. Healthcare. We **take** these things **for granted**, but for much of the world's population, they're in short supply. Some 1.4 billion people live in extreme **poverty**, **barely surviving** on $1.25 per day. In certain regions, like sub-Saharan Africa, South Asia, and Latin America,
5 not only is poverty widespread, but it's passed on from generation to generation. Research on the **complex** problem has identified several keys to breaking the poverty cycle.

   Diseases like AIDS, malaria, and tuberculosis are among the greatest **burdens** on the poor. Some 40 million people are **infected** with AIDS, and
10 95% of all cases are in the developing world. Malaria, rampant in parts of Africa, has an economic cost of $12 billion a year due to medical costs and lost work. And, tuberculosis continues to sicken millions. Efforts are underway to
15 **stamp out** these diseases, such as groups distributing anti-malaria bed nets. Critical medicines and **vaccines** are also being provided by the UN, government agencies, and NGOs. Breaking this link
20 in the poverty cycle is a top **priority**.

Vaccination programs save lives by preventing diseases before they hit.

   Education is another key area, as knowledge, skills, and training can help families improve their lives through higher earnings. Poor nations often **lack** the resources to fund universal education or adult literacy programs. However, there are success stories. In Mozambique and Bolivia, money
25 saved from national debt relief programs has been **channeled** into education systems. In a related issue, there is a critical link between **nutrition** and education. Many poor children are undernourished, with a

---

⁴ sub-Saharan – south of the Sahara Desert
⁸ malaria – a disease spread by mosquito bites
⁸ tuberculosis – a disease affecting the lungs
¹⁹ NGO – non-governmental organization (ex: Doctors Without Borders)
²³ universal – available to everybody
²³ literacy – the ability to read
²⁵ debt relief – the limiting or canceling of a debt load
²⁶ critical – very important

lack of iron and iodine leading to stunted brain development. Thus, along with being well taught, children must also be well fed.

30 Improving economic conditions, both on the local and national level, is another part of the **equation**. Families with more resources eat better, get better medical care, and have access to more resources. On the local level, there has been success with micro-loans. As the name suggests, these are small
35 loans to people and **communities** to start businesses and enhance infrastructure. In Thailand, for example, the government provides micro-loans of $100-$300 to farmers and street vendors for seeds,
40 equipment, and goods.

Micro-credit programs allow poor people to go into business.

On the national level, a number of countries, including Vietnam and Malaysia, have brought poverty levels down by producing more goods locally. They're also pushing to increase exports to wealthy countries. Yet
45 observers say rich countries make this difficult, as their import tariffs and subsidies act as market barriers. This is especially the case with agricultural goods.

Without question, poor countries face complex, interconnected challenges. In addition to the above problems, others, such as corruption, war, and
50 gender inequality, come into play. Despite the bad news, there have been success stories. In East Asia, the poverty rate fell from 80% in 1981 to 18% in 2005. And, one of the UN's Millennium Development Goals is to halve global poverty rates by 2015. With governments and aid groups working together, we can hopefully end the cycle of poverty, one family at a time.

28 stunted – restricted; limited
36 infrastructure – basic services, such as roads, bridges, power lines, etc.
45 tariff – fee to import or export goods
46 subsidies – payments made by governments to local businesses to support them
50 gender inequality – unequal treatment of men and women
50 come into play – enter into the situation
52 millennium – period of 1,000 years

Choose the best answer.

.... **Main Idea**

1. (   ) What is the main idea?
   A. Increasing international trade is the best way to end poverty.
   B. Poverty in rich countries is not passed on from parents to children.
   C. To reduce poverty, a number of key issues must be addressed.
   D. The UN is an important organization in the fight against poverty.

.... **Detail**

2. (   ) How much did the poverty rate in East Asia fall from 1981 to 2005?
   A. 18%
   B. 62%
   C. 80%
   D. 95%

.... **Vocabulary**

3. (   ) In line 36, what does "enhance" mean?
   A. employ   B. draft
   C. yearn   D. improve

.... **Analysis**

4. (   ) Which of these people would be a good candidate for a micro-loan?
   A. A man who is planning to buy a new car
   B. A villager who needs a cart to bring his goods to market
   C. A restaurant owner who wants to open a third branch
   D. A woman who wants to buy a house

5. (   ) Why do poor countries have trouble selling goods to rich countries?
   A. Transportation issues are hard to solve.
   B. There are trade barriers in place.
   C. The standard of local goods is low.
   D. Poor countries have high import tariffs.

Short Answers **Answer each question based on the article.**

1. Worldwide, how many people live in extreme poverty?

_____

2. What are three serious diseases affecting poor countries?

_____

3. How can poor nutrition affect a child's development?

_____

Vocabulary Building

A **Choose the answer that means the same as the word or phrase in italics.**

1. As rents rose to unaffordable levels, the *burden* was too great for many low-income residents.
   A. difficulty   B. interest   C. greed

2. With only one day in New York City, we'll *barely* have enough time to see the Statue of Liberty and Museum of Modern Art.
   A. certainly   B. hurriedly   C. scarcely

3. Our marketers recommend *channeling* 80% of spending into television ads.
   A. viewing   B. respecting   C. directing

4. The police commissioner promises to *stamp out* departmental waste.
   A. eliminate   B. estimate   C. equate

5. During economic downturns, small companies *survive* by cutting all but the most essential costs.
   A. expand   B. continue   C. supply

B **Complete each sentence with the best word or phrase. Remember to use the correct word form.**

poverty	community	take for granted	equation	lack

1. One advantage of living near a river is you'll never _____ fresh water.

2. We can't _____ that this good weather will last all week.

3. Leaders of the _____ are calling for a lower speed limit.

4. As they're living in _____, the family hasn't got the money to take their child to a doctor.

5. To make a neighborhood safer, more street lights and police patrols are an important part of the _____.

C **Circle the correct form of each word.**

1. Not only is fruit salad (nutrition/nutritious), but it tastes great.

2. The (complexity/complex) of the novel is one of its strengths.

3. Let's (priority/prioritize) the tasks by deciding which ones need to be handled first.

4. Thanks to a UN program, the entire village will be (vaccinated/vaccination) against polio.

5. You can't catch the disease from him since it isn't (infected/infectious).

Part 2: Focus Areas

Focus on Language

Word Parts

Study the word parts in the chart. Then, read the following pairs of sentences. Circle if the second sentence is true or false.

Word Part	Meaning	Examples
en-	cause	encourage, enact
-equ-	same	unequal, equilibrium
-ness	state or condition	tenderness, shyness

1. Seeing the fox threaten the cubs enraged the mother bear.
   The bear was angered by the fox. (True / False)

2. As the payment amount was inadequate, the goods haven't been shipped.
   Not enough money was sent for the items. (True / False)

3. Mr. Tran is known for his forgetfulness, so I always remind him of meetings.
   Mr. Tran always remembers the meeting times. (True / False)

Grammar *Along with, Besides, & In addition to*

> These three prepositions are used to provide more information about something. They're followed by a noun (quite often a gerund) to form a prepositional phrase.
>
> Ex: Along with being an excellent value, the lunch specials are delicious.
>
> Ex: Besides showing me around Paris, Jacques taught me some French.
>
> Ex: The store sells antique maps in addition to used books.

Combine the two sentences using the preposition in parentheses.

1. Bill Gates is Microsoft's founder. He's also involved in charity work. (Besides)

   _____

2. The children need new shoes. They also need new jackets. (In addition to)

   _____

3. Jacky manages our finances. He also oversees the IT department. (along with)

   _____

Talk About It   **Discuss these questions in small groups.**

1. In the world's poorest countries, who is to blame for widespread poverty? The government? Businesses? Someone else?

2. In your country, is the gap between the rich and poor growing, shrinking, or staying the same?

3. How do you see the future? Will the situation improve or worsen for the world's poor?

Write About It

Question: In your opinion, what are the keys to breaking the poverty cycle? List three ideas. Prepare by writing notes on the lines below. The first few words of the paragraph are written to help you get started.

Idea 1: _____

Idea 2: _____

Idea 3: _____

In order to break the poverty cycle, _____

_____

_____

_____

_____

_____

_____

_____

_____

Listening

Listen to the conversation. Then, answer the following questions.

Track 59

1. ( ) Why does the woman want to speak with the man?
   (A) To ask a favor   (B) To return an item
   (C) To make an apology   (D) To offer advice

2. ( ) Who is in charge of the community center?
   (A) Brenda   (B) Ms. Jefferson
   (C) Ricky   (D) Mr. Lewis

3. ( ) Why does the woman have trouble looking after her brother?
   (A) She works full-time.
   (B) She is on a basketball team.
   (C) She has schoolwork.
   (D) She helps her mother all day.

Reading

Read the article. Then, answer the following questions.

In the fight against infectious diseases, non-governmental organizations (NGOs) play a crucial role. These private groups work independently or in cooperation with the United Nations, local governments, and international aid organizations like the Red Cross. They're funded by donations and staffed by full-time and volunteer workers.

One of the most well known (and most generous) is the Bill & Melinda Gates Foundation, set up by Microsoft founder Bill Gates. The organization has spent billions of dollars providing vaccines and health care in the effort to stamp out diseases like tuberculosis. In sub-Saharan Africa and South Asia, where hundreds of millions live in poverty, groups like this are not just making headlines – they're saving lives.

1. ( ) What is the main topic of this article?
   (A) Poverty in South Asia   (B) The role of NGOs in fighting disease
   (C) The world's richest man   (D) Donation drives for the Red Cross

2. ( ) What can be inferred about the Gates Foundation?
   (A) It's the world's oldest NGO.
   (B) Its efforts have saved many lives.
   (C) Its headquarters are in Asia.
   (D) It's part of the United Nations.

3. ( ) The word "crucial" in paragraph 1, line 2, is closest in meaning to
   (A) artificial   (B) suspenseful
   (C) essential   (D) analytical

Supplementary Reading - *Banker to the Poor* Track 60

Micro-loans allow people with little or no credit to borrow money. The father of the concept is Dr. Muhammad Yunus, an economist from Bangladesh. Dr. Yunus' innovation was born out of dire necessity. In the early 1970s, as he taught economics at Chittagong University, he witnessed the terrible famine affecting his country. Frustrated at the disparity between the economics he taught and the real-world situation, he set his mind to changing things.

Recognizing that credit is the lifeblood of an economy, Dr. Yunus hit upon the idea of micro-loans. He started by lending his own money, in very small amounts, to the poorest of the poor. Then, in 1983 he started Grameen Bank to expand his efforts. Most borrowers are women, and they have to show that they own less than one-half acre of land. The small loans (usually less than $200) are used to open shops, buy seeds, and fund small enterprises. Over the years, Grameen Bank has loaned more than $8 billion to poor Bangladeshis and has expanded to over 1,000 branches in Bangladesh. Overwhelmingly, borrowers have shown their credit-worthiness, with a solid 98% repaying their loans.

In his book *Banker to the Poor*, Dr. Yunus discusses his experiences leading to the founding of Grameen Bank. His micro-credit model has been put into practice by banks in more than 100 countries. For his tireless efforts on behalf of the poor, Dr. Yunus has received numerous awards, including the Nikkei Asia Prize for Regional Growth in 2004 and the Nobel Peace Prize in 2006.

Read each sentence. Circle if it is true (T) or false (F).

1. The majority of Grameen Bank's customers are women.   T / F
2. Grameen Bank hired Dr. Yunus because of his economics background. T / F
3. Dr. Yunus won the Nobel Peace Prize before the Nikkei Asia Prize.   T / F
4. About 2% of the loans made by Grameen Bank are repaid in full.   T / F
5. Micro-credit systems can be found in more than 100 countries.   T / F

16 The Future

The Future of Energy

For many years, fossil fuels like oil and coal have powered our factories, brought electricity to our homes, and fueled our cars. Yet these energy sources have serious economic and environmental shortcomings. In response, countries are supporting clean energy sources, which will power the future.

Pre-Reading Questions Discuss these questions in pairs.

1. What is the problem with burning fossil fuels for energy?

2. What are some "clean" energy sources? (ex: solar energy)

3. Besides gas-powered cars, what other kinds of cars are on the market?

Vocabulary Warmup Track 61

A **Listen to the unit's target vocabulary. Then, write the letter of the correct word or phrase next to each definition.**

a. abundant	f. efficient	k. moreover
b. acquire	g. electricity	l. rural
c. alternative	h. fossil fuel	m. transition
d. at a crossroads	i. gradually	n. underground
e. combination	j. manufacture	o. used up

___ 1. in the countryside

___ 2. spent; emptied

___ 3. carbon-based energy source (ex: oil and coal)

___ 4. change; shift

___ 5. make; create

___ 6. get; pick up

___ 7. substitute; other option

___ 8. beneath the Earth

___ 9. slowly; over time

___ 10. group; two or more things put together

B **Complete each sentence with a target word or phrase. Remember to use the correct word form.**

1. Planting a garden is a great hobby. _____, it's a way to get fresh, nutritious vegetables.

2. To save _____, turn off the lights when you leave the room.

3. We're _____, and it's time to decide whether to go public or stay private.

4. As the research group is connected to a university, it has a(n) _____ supply of volunteers for its experiments.

5. Karen is so _____ that she can finish a task in half the time it takes most people.

153

Part 1: Reading and Vocabulary Building

Reading Passage 🔘 Track 62

1   The world is **at a crossroads**. We currently get 90% of our energy from **fossil fuels** like oil and coal. However, those resources, besides being limited, are a leading cause of global warming. At the same time, a revolution in clean energy is underway. "**Alternative**" energy sources
5   like solar and wind power are receiving sizeable investments. And, related advances in technology are promising to make our homes and cities cleaner.

Renewable energy sources are leading the way, since they're clean and can never be **used up**. One of these, sunlight, is a perfect example, as it's
10 both widespread and free. Furthermore, solar panels, used to transform sunlight into electricity, have become more **efficient** and cheaper to **manufacture** in recent years. Asia is a leader in the
15 field, with both China and India aiming to produce 20 gigawatts of solar power by 2020. The countries have huge **rural** areas that aren't connected to the main power grids. Yet once solar panels are
20 installed, they can immediately start generating their own **electricity**.

Installing solar panels on the roof of one's home is a growing practice.

Rural areas are also excellent places to generate wind power, another renewable energy source. "Wind farms" are made up of wind turbines which produce electricity as they're spun by the wind. The potential for this type of operation is impressive, as the electricity from a single
25 turbine can power 500 households. **Moreover**, unused energy can be sold to power companies, an advantage also shared by solar generators. However, care needs to be taken with the placement of turbines. In

---

⁴ revolution – extreme change
⁸ renewable – able to be used and reused over and over
¹¹ solar panel – sheet that captures sunlight so it can be converted into electricity
¹⁶ gigawatt – one billion watts of electrical power
¹⁹ power grid – system that distributes electricity throughout an area
²² wind turbine – a tall pole with long blades that generate electricity by being
       spun by the wind

addition to being eyesores, they can pose a danger to migrating birds.

30 Many other alternative energy sources are being developed. The most common is hydroelectric power, with electricity produced by falling water (usually at dams). Other renewable sources include

35 geothermal power (from **underground** steam), wave power (from ocean waves), and biofuel (from biological matter like plants). Based on their local resources, many countries are investing in one or more of these technologies. For instance, Norway and Brazil,

40 with **abundant** water resources, already get most of their electricity from hydroelectric power.

Wind farms are quiet, efficient, and easy to maintain.

Typically, alternative energy sources are used to generate electricity for factories, homes, and other buildings. The automobile industry, because of its heavy reliance on fossil fuels, is also receiving special attention. For

45 years, hybrid cars, which use a **combination** of gasoline and electricity, have been in production. All-electric cars are also being made, and the use of ethanol (a type of biofuel) is growing. Furthermore, there's strong interest in using hydrogen to power cars through the use of "fuel cells." This pollution-free power source was used decades ago in the spaceships

50 that carried people to the moon.

Many countries are aiming to **acquire** 10-20% of their energy from renewable sources by 2020. However, it's likely we'll continue relying on fossil fuels for several decades to come. As the costs of fossil fuels rise and alternative energy costs fall, countries will **gradually** make the **transition**

55 to renewable sources. As that happens, government investment will likely be key in developing the energy sources of the future.

[28] eyesore – something that is unpleasant to look at
[28] pose – present; cause
[29] migrating – traveling a long distance (ex: birds migrating south in the winter)
[34] dam – structure that controls water flow, often for electricity production
[43] automobile – vehicle such as a car or truck
[48] fuel cell – device that converts sources like hydrogen into usable energy

.... **Main Idea**

1. ( ) What is the main idea?
   A. For our power needs, renewable energy is growing in importance.
   B. In the future, most of our energy will come from solar power.
   C. Alternative energy sources will replace fossil fuels within a decade.
   D. Global warming is caused by burning fossil fuels like coal and oil.

.... **Detail**

2. ( ) What energy source would two tons of food waste be used for?
   A. Geothermal power
   B. Biofuel
   C. Hydroelectric power
   D. Wave power

.... **Vocabulary**

3. ( ) In line 5, what does "sizeable" mean?
   A. substantial   B. parallel
   C. attainable   D. alternative

.... **Analysis**

4. ( ) What can be inferred about solar panels?
   A. They work more efficiently in urban areas than in rural areas.
   B. They can produce a maximum of 20 gigawatts of power.
   C. They are used to transform electricity into sunlight.
   D. They don't need to be connected to the main power grid.

5. ( ) What does the article suggest about fossil fuels?
   A. They will still provide us with power dozens of years from now.
   B. They will continue to cost the same for decades to come.
   C. They will get cheaper as other fuels become more popular.
   D. They will suffer a fall in quality as their quantities decrease.

Short Answers **Answer each question based on the article.**

1. How many homes can be powered by a wind turbine?

   _____

2. Besides being renewable, what do solar and wind power have in common?

   _____

3. What are two types of fuel (besides gasoline) which may power future cars?

   _____

Vocabulary Building

A **Choose the answer that means the same as the word or phrase in italics.**

1. The *abundant* flower grows all over the hillside.
   A. beautiful   B. plentiful   C. seasonal

2. The company is Japanese, but the cars are *manufactured* in the USA.
   A. licensed   B. produced   C. distributed

3. *Acquiring* so many cranes for the building project will take time.
   A. Directing   B. Building   C. Obtaining

4. The *transition* from print to digital format took the magazine's readers a few months to get used to.
   A. discussion   B. comprehension   C. conversion

5. During the expedition to the North Pole, most of the supplies were *used up* in the first two weeks.
   A. spent   B. misplaced   C. frozen

B **Complete each sentence with the best word or phrase. Remember to use the correct word form.**

| underground | moreover | fossil fuel | rural | at a crossroads |

1. Dr. Mullin is an expert in solar energy. _____, she's knowledgeable about wind power.

2. Stephen says he's _____. He can either move to France to study art or go into business with his brother.

3. The problem with living in a(n) _____ area is it takes so long to drive anywhere.

4. Coal, a common _____, has been widely used for centuries.

5. They're digging holes in the area in search of _____ water.

C **Circle the correct form of each word.**

1. They can't improve the (efficient/efficiency) of the factory without buying new equipment.

2. (Alternatively/Alternative), we could go hiking instead of skiing.

3. By (combining/combination) comedy and action, the movie appeals to several types of movie goers.

4. So much (electric/electricity) is used here that you can see the city from space.

5. Over the last 50 years, there has been a (gradual/gradually) population shift from small towns to cities.

Part 2: Focus Areas

Focus on Language

Word Parts

Study the word parts in the chart. Then, read the following pairs of sentences. Circle if the second sentence is true or false.

Word Part	Meaning	Examples
alter-	other	alternator, alterable
-fac(t)-	make	artifact, faction
-ent	in a certain state	latent, complacent

1. The two security guards alternate working weekend shifts.
   Both of the guards work every weekend. (True / False)

2. There was so much dissatisfaction with the brand that it was discontinued.
   Many people were unhappy with the brand. (True / False)

3. It's a potent medicine which is only prescribed in serious cases.
   Doctors recommend the medicine to patients with mild symptoms. (True / False)

Grammar *Used to*

The phrase "used to" can be confusing because of its variety of uses. It can describe something that was once true but no longer is. Or, it can describe something that you are accustomed to. The phrase can also explain something's purpose.

Type 1: Past situation	Ex: She used to work as a lab technician.
Type 2: Be accustomed to	Ex: We're used to living through hot summers.
Type 3: Purpose	Ex: This tool is used to separate pieces of metal.

Rewrite each sentence using *used to*. The first few words are given.

1. On the website, you can plan many events, including weddings and parties.
   The website can be _____

2. Years ago, I lived in Taichung, but now I live in Hualien.
   I used to _____

3. Dealing with angry customers is something I'm accustomed to.
   I'm used to _____

Talk About It   **Discuss these questions in small groups.**

1. In your country, which types of clean energy are the most practical? Are your resources better suited for solar, wind, or another renewable source?

2. In general, are people willing to pay more for products (like electric cars) that are better for the environment? Or, do they usually make decisions based on price?

3. Are you worried about global warming? Is enough being done to slow the problem down?

Write About It

Question: How can governments convince companies to stop getting energy from fossil fuels and start using clean energy sources? Give three ideas. Prepare by writing notes on the lines below. The first few words of the paragraph are written to help you get started.

Idea 1: _____

Idea 2: _____

Idea 3: _____

If governments want companies to switch to clean energy sources,

_____

_____

_____

_____

_____

_____

_____

Listening

Track 63

Listen to the report. Then, answer the following questions.

1. (   ) What is the main purpose of this report?
    (A) To introduce some alternative energy sources
    (B) To discuss this year's corn harvest
    (C) To announce an important research advance
    (D) To criticize a type of biofuel

2. (   ) Why are some people opposed to ethanol?
    (A) It affects food prices.   (B) It's expensive.
    (C) It's hard to produce.   (D) It isn't clean.

3. (   ) What is suggested about the future?
    (A) Supporters of ethanol will win the debate.
    (B) Corn supplies will run out fairly soon.
    (C) Determining the food/energy balance will be easy.
    (D) People will continue criticizing ethanol.

Reading   **Choose the correct word(s) to fill in each blank.**

Batteries supply electricity to (___1___) devices, yet their disposal can be problematic. Long ago, most portable devices used disposable batteries. Unfortunately, in addition to taking up landfill space, batteries are not biodegradable. Moreover, they can leak toxic chemicals into the soil, contaminating the land for thousands of years. Over time, more machines, like computers and cameras, came (___2___) pre-installed with rechargeable power supplies. For other devices using common battery sizes, rechargeable batteries became widely available. Yet cost and performance issues limited their popularity. The latest (___3___) of rechargeable batteries hold their charge and last longer. Though they still cost more than disposable batteries, they can be reused hundreds of times. Every type of battery, after it can no longer be used, should be recycled.

1. (   ) (A) countable   (B) counting
         (C) counted   (D) countless

2. (   ) (A) to be   (B) have been
         (C) be   (D) been

3. (   ) (A) generations   (B) alterations
         (C) summations   (D) gradations

Supplementary Reading - *Iceland's Energy Future* Track 64

As the world transitions from fossil fuels to renewable energy sources, some countries will get there faster than others. Due to its small population and rich natural resources, Iceland is uniquely positioned to make a rapid crossover. The country has abundant renewable energy sources, allowing it to meet most of its electricity and heating needs through the generation of hydroelectric and geothermal power.

Next on the agenda are the nation's automobiles. Of the roughly 300,000 residents, most rely on private cars for transportation. However, imported oil is expensive, making it costly to operate cars and fishing boats. Gas burning engines dominate, but that's starting to change. Since 2003, the capital Reykjavik (home to more than one-third of the population) has had a hydrogen refueling station. Over time, the number of stations is expected to grow.

The world's largest automakers have taken an interest in Iceland's progressive energy policies. GM, Toyota, and others have put prototype fuel cell vehicles on the road in Reykjavik to see how they'll operate in real-world driving conditions. As these companies compete for the world's rapidly growing clean energy market, such feedback will be invaluable.

Iceland is well positioned to become the first "hydrogen economy," which is in fact the official government policy. The country's energy production is already so advanced that it's marketing the advantage to foreign companies. Many firms, such as data storage firms, use large amounts of electricity. They may soon find themselves relocating to the remote island to save a fortune on energy costs.

Read each sentence. Circle if it is true (T) or false (F).

1. Hydroelectric and geothermal sources supply Iceland with energy.   T / F
2. More than 100,000 people live in Reykjavik.   T / F
3. In the future, Iceland's capital will likely have more hydrogen refueling stations.   T / F
4. Fuel cell cars are currently being driven in Reykjavik.   T / F
5. Iceland plans to export its electricity to foreign countries.   T / F

Target Vocabulary List

☐ decline	Unit 5	☐ expert	Unit 1
☐ defend	Unit 9	☐ expressive	Unit 2
☐ depression	Unit 13	☐ extensively	Unit 13
☐ device	Unit 13	☐ fall into a habit	Unit 8
☐ dim	Unit 4	☐ fierce	Unit 9
☐ disabled	Unit 12	☐ file for bankruptcy	Unit 8
☐ discover	Unit 1	☐ flexibility	Unit 13
☐ drive up	Unit 11	☐ fossil fuel	Unit 16
☐ eager	Unit 5	☐ fraud	Unit 11
☐ ecosystem	Unit 9	☐ from scratch	Unit 3
☐ efficient	Unit 16	☐ frustrated	Unit 7
☐ effort	Unit 3	☐ functional	Unit 6
☐ electricity	Unit 16	☐ generate	Unit 3
☐ embarrassment	Unit 2	☐ gesture	Unit 2
☐ emit	Unit 9	☐ gradually	Unit 16
☐ encourage	Unit 2	☐ graphics	Unit 10
☐ enemy	Unit 9	☐ hygiene	Unit 7
☐ enforce	Unit 7	☐ ideal	Unit 13
☐ engineer	Unit 12	☐ identity	Unit 6
☐ enormous	Unit 8	☐ imagination	Unit 6
☐ entrepreneur	Unit 12	☐ impact	Unit 6
☐ equation	Unit 15	☐ in order to	Unit 10
☐ essential	Unit 7	☐ in the meantime	Unit 14
☐ estimate	Unit 11	☐ indirect	Unit 4
☐ eventually	Unit 6	☐ infected	Unit 15
☐ evidence	Unit 1	☐ inhabited	Unit 4
☐ examine	Unit 4	☐ in-house	Unit 5
☐ excess	Unit 3	☐ innovative	Unit 5
☐ executive	Unit 11	☐ inspection	Unit 7
☐ exhausted	Unit 10	☐ instrument	Unit 1

☐	integrate	Unit 10	☐	opponent	Unit 10
☐	intended for	Unit 11	☐	opportunity	Unit 3
☐	intensely	Unit 2	☐	opposite	Unit 2
☐	interact	Unit 13	☐	organ	Unit 9
☐	lack	Unit 15	☐	organize	Unit 1
☐	landmark	Unit 6	☐	out of hand	Unit 10
☐	layout	Unit 9	☐	overhaul	Unit 11
☐	leap over	Unit 6	☐	perception	Unit 9
☐	legend	Unit 8	☐	phenomenon	Unit 13
☐	lifestyle	Unit 8	☐	physics	Unit 14
☐	limitation	Unit 4	☐	policy	Unit 3
☐	locate	Unit 4	☐	posture	Unit 2
☐	loyalty	Unit 5	☐	potential	Unit 3
☐	made up of	Unit 14	☐	pour in	Unit 1
☐	maintain	Unit 5	☐	poverty	Unit 15
☐	make the most of	Unit 10	☐	practical	Unit 14
☐	manufacture	Unit 16	☐	predictable	Unit 13
☐	masterpiece	Unit 6	☐	preserve	Unit 6
☐	mineral	Unit 9	☐	previously	Unit 11
☐	modify	Unit 12	☐	priority	Unit 15
☐	more often than not	Unit 5	☐	prison	Unit 11
☐	moreover	Unit 16	☐	productive	Unit 12
☐	mortgage	Unit 8	☐	raw material	Unit 3
☐	multiple	Unit 14	☐	realistic	Unit 10
☐	muscle	Unit 2	☐	recipient	Unit 11
☐	no wonder	Unit 1	☐	reckless	Unit 8
☐	not to mention	Unit 7	☐	refer to	Unit 2
☐	nutrition	Unit 15	☐	refuse	Unit 12
☐	obliged	Unit 8	☐	regardless of	Unit 5
☐	occur	Unit 7	☐	region	Unit 1

☐ reluctant	Unit 12		☐ symbol	Unit 6
☐ remind	Unit 1		☐ take for granted	Unit 15
☐ revenue	Unit 6		☐ take notice	Unit 3
☐ role	Unit 1		☐ technique	Unit 4
☐ roughly	Unit 8		☐ tend to	Unit 2
☐ ruin	Unit 11		☐ theoretical	Unit 14
☐ rural	Unit 16		☐ touch down	Unit 9
☐ scandal	Unit 7		☐ track	Unit 1
☐ senior citizen	Unit 13		☐ transaction	Unit 14
☐ sequence	Unit 2		☐ transition	Unit 16
☐ severe	Unit 11		☐ underground	Unit 16
☐ shocking	Unit 7		☐ underway	Unit 4
☐ shrink	Unit 14		☐ unemployment rate	Unit 12
☐ signal	Unit 4		☐ unfounded	Unit 12
☐ simultaneous	Unit 14		☐ unique	Unit 1
☐ slightly	Unit 4		☐ universe	Unit 4
☐ society	Unit 12		☐ upkeep	Unit 8
☐ sophisticated	Unit 11		☐ used up	Unit 16
☐ spectacular	Unit 9		☐ vaccine	Unit 15
☐ sponsor	Unit 10		☐ vary	Unit 2
☐ stamp out	Unit 15		☐ vast	Unit 9
☐ stand for	Unit 6		☐ vessel	Unit 9
☐ state of affairs	Unit 7		☐ victim	Unit 11
☐ strategy	Unit 5		☐ violate	Unit 7
☐ struggling	Unit 6		☐ visual	Unit 12
☐ submit	Unit 5		☐ widespread	Unit 3
☐ suitable	Unit 4		☐ wind up	Unit 8
☐ superb	Unit 14		☐ work ethic	Unit 12
☐ survey	Unit 8		☐ worthless	Unit 3
☐ survive	Unit 15		☐ yield	Unit 14

About the Author

Andrew E. Bennett holds an EdM (Master of Education) degree from Harvard University and a BA degree from UC Santa Cruz. He has studied seven languages. It's a life-long passion that began with a study of Spanish and continues with his ongoing studies of Chinese and Japanese.

Andrew has been involved in English education since 1993, both as a teacher and a writer. He has taught a variety of subjects, including English composition, business writing, English literature, and TOEFL preparation.

Andrew is the author of more than 30 English learning books, including classroom texts, supplementary books, self-study books, as well as TOEIC preparation texts. In addition to writing and teaching, he regularly attends ESL conferences and gives presentations to groups of teachers at schools and symposiums.

Central to Andrew's teaching philosophy is an emphasis on content. His work includes subjects from countries around the world, giving his writing an international flavor. Andrew also enjoys writing about cultural issues, as he is convinced of the vital link between language and culture.